Famous Biographies for Young People

FAMOUS POETS FOR YOUNG PEOPLE

by Laura Benét

ILLUSTRATED

2.24

Dodd, Mead & Company · New York

Sixth Printing

Printed in the United States of America
by Vail-Ballou Press, Inc., Binghamton, N. Y.

Acknowledgment is gratefully made to the holders of copyright for the use
of the following material: *Children and Books* by May Hill Arbuthnot,
copyright 1947 by Scott Foresman and Company. *The Poet of Christmas Eve*
by Samuel White Patterson, copyright 1956 by Morehouse-Gorham. *Edward
Lear* by Angus Davidson, copyright 1939. *A Book of Nonsense*, copyright
1862 by Routledge, Warne and Routledge, London. *Lewis Carroll* by Derek
Hudson, copyright 1954 by Constable, London, and *Through the Looking-
Glass* by Lewis Carroll, copyright 1902 by Harper. *Those Innocent Years*,
copyright 1957 by Bobbs Merrill Company, and *The Complete Poetical
Works* of James Whitcomb Riley, copyright 1937 by the Bobbs Merrill
Company. *Stepping Westward* by Laura E. Richards, copyright 1931 by
D. Appleton and Company. *Tirra Lirra* by Laura E. Richards, copyright
1902 by Dana Estes and Company. *The Strange Case of Robert Louis Steven-
son* by Malcolm Elwin, copyright 1950 by Macdonald, London. *A Child's
Garden of Verses* by Robert Louis Stevenson, copyright 1885 by Longman's
Green Inc., London. *The Gay Poet. A Life of Eugene Field* by Jeanette
Covert Nolan, copyright 1940, Messner. *Hilaire Belloc. An Anthology of
his Prose and Verse*, Selected by W. N. Roughead, copyright 1951 by Rupert
Hart Davis, London. *Hilaire Belloc* by Robert Speaight, copyright 1957 by
Farrar, Straus and Cudahy. *The Junior Book of Authors*, copyright 1951 by
the H. W. Wilson Company. *British Authors of the Nineteenth Century*,
copyright 1936 by H. W. Wilson Company. *Peacock Pie* by Walter de la
Mare, copyright 1913 by Henry Holt and Company. *The West-going Heart:
A Life of Vachel Lindsay* by Eleanor Ruggles, copyright 1959 by W. W.
Norton and Company. *Water Babies* by Charles Kingsley, copyright 1863 by
Macmillan and Company, London. *Herself and the Houseful* by Thomas
Augustine Daly, copyright 1924 by Harcourt Brace and Company. Permis-
sion from Harcourt Brace and Company to use Mr. Daly's poem, "Carlotta's
Indecision" from *Canzoni*, copyright 1906 by *Philadelphia Catholic Standard
Times*. To J. B. Lippincott for permission to use "The Night Will Never
Stay" from *Poems for Children* by Eleanor Farjeon, copyright 1951. To
E. P. Dutton and Company for permission to use a stanza of A. A. Milne's
poem, "They Are Changing the Guard at Buckingham Palace" from the
book *When We Were Very Young*, by A. A. Milne, copyright 1924 by
E. P. Dutton & Company, Inc. *Autobiography* by A. A. Milne, copyright
1939 by A. A. Milne. To Macmillan and Company for permission to use a

To the lovely and loving

K. A.

who gave such joy

(Kathleen Anne Benét Fry)
1917–1962

FOREWORD

Children have an instinctive response to motion and rhythm. Many sing tunes before they know words and bounce and dance instead of walking, especially when they hear a hurdy-gurdy. There is a true love of poetry in most children if it is given a chance to grow. Curiosity and imagination are stimulated by an acquaintance with the great poets who have written for children.

The aim of this book has been to gather together the poets who have made significant contributions to children's literature: William Blake whose "The Lamb" is so well known; William Allingham with his classic of the little people, "The Fairies"; Charles Kingsley and "The Lost Doll"; De la Mare who gave us "Peacock Pie"; Robert Louis Stevenson who wrote *A Child's Garden of Verses*—Eleanor Farjeon, Rachel Field, and others among our later poets. A child recognizes the best. Even though the words are new to him a child will grasp the mood. He may touch an unfamiliar world through a new vision of the familiar world around him that poets such as Stevenson have described with such genius.

Lucky are children if they have learned songs and ballads at their mother's knee, for such chiming music will stay with them as long as they live. It is like the ringing of bells.

CONTENTS

Illustrations follow page 64

9

CONTENTS

MOTHER GOOSE

MOTHER GOOSE, that dear, jolly old dame, comforter and entertainer of our youthful days, seems as familar as a well-loved aunt or grandmother. Yet her identity has never been proved or her place of residence fully established. France, England, America all claim her. She is truly a legend. Her name was given to *Mother Goose's Melodies* published as a chapbook for children by Thomas Fleet of Boston, Massachusetts, and supposed to be her first appearance. A copy of the eleventh edition shows the date 1719. But this story is discounted because *Children And Books* by May Hill Arbuthnot, says Perrault's *Contes De La Mère L'Oye* (*Tales of My Mother Goose*) appeared in 1697. Its frontispiece was an old woman telling stories to an interested group of children. Upon a placard by her side was lettered the title:

> Contes
> de Ma
> Mère
> l'Oye

Some would even go further back and mingle French legend with history. They would claim that the mother of Charlemagne who bore the title of Queen Goose-foot was the only true source. In any case, France, not America, is the cradle of the famous nursery rhymes.

The next mention of the name in England is in connection with John Newbery. He brought out the collection of nursery rhymes called *Mother Goose's Melody Or Sonnets For The Cradle.* Leigh Hunt says of the Newbery books that "they were certain little penny books—radiant with gold and rich with bad pictures."

The first American edition was issued by Isaiah Thomas, a publisher of Worcester, Massachusetts. W. H. Whitmore reproduced the book in full in 1889, calling it the *Original Mother Goose's Melody.* Certainly the jolliest story of them all is that of Elizabeth Vergoose (née Foster) of Boston. William A. Wheeler edited a charming volume of *Mother Goose's Melodies* and in it identified the famous Mother Goose with Elizabeth Vergoose. She was without doubt the Mother Goose of America.

Wherever the rhymes originated, they have provided for every contingency of childhood—food and drink, pets domestic and otherwise, winter and summer sports, disasters, weather. Who does not remember this description of a cold day?

> My mother and your mother
> Went over the way.
> Said my mother to your mother
> It's chop-a-nose day.

And what more fearsome mystery story could one conceive than that of the goosey gander who found the old man who wouldn't say his prayers in a lonely bedchamber and treated him so brutally? Or what better solution could be found for two perverse cranks than the meal of Jack Sprat and his wife? Many of these rhymes are believed to have a political origin and to have been satirical in their meaning. Whatever their hidden implications, we could never do without Mother Goose, wherever she originated. She is a boon and a blessing. The child soon discovers that these Mother Goose rhymes skip, gallop, walk, run, swing, trot and leap just as music does. Saying these verses, a child gets a happy introduction to rhyme. Here is a rhyme that is much more like a lyric than a jingle and a good one to wind up with:

> I had a little nut tree, nothing would it bear
> But a silver apple and a golden pear;
> The King of Spain's daughter came to visit me,
> And all for the sake of my little nut tree.
> I skipped over water, I danced over sea,
> And all the birds in the air couldn't catch me.

WILLIAM BLAKE

[1757–1827]

As a boy, the poet William Blake was a strange lad with remarkable gifts. He was born in London, England, on November 28, 1757, the second of five children. His father, James Blake, had a small hosier's shop in that city, and until Blake was grown he lived with his family in rooms over the shop. For the most part he was a gentle, amiable child but sometimes showed violent temper when roused. All his life he saw visions, beginning when he was only four years old. At that age he saw God's face looking in at him through the window. A few years later at Peckham Rye he saw a tree filled with angels. He told his mother he had seen and talked with the prophet Ezekiel and she punished him for telling what she thought was a lie. As a man he insisted that he spoke with those who were gone and they guided him. So people began to call him "Mad Blake."

As a little boy he was taught at home but showed such unusual talent for drawing that his father made a great effort and sent him to Henry Par's drawing school. Though only ten years old, young Blake worked devotedly at his drawing and constantly visited the exhibitions and shops of London's great art dealers. These men used to encourage him to talk

about the prints and nicknamed him "the little connoisseur."
At fourteen he was apprenticed to a famous engraver named
James Basire who apparently understood the odd boy. But
other boys made fun of him and his temper got him into fights.

After an apprenticeship of seven years, Blake at twenty-one
studied at the Royal Academy. At twenty-five he married
Catherine Boucher whose father was a market gardener. She
had had no education, so he taught her to read and write and
their marriage was a happy one. For a time they prospered.
The rising artists of the day knew Blake and he would recite
and sing his own compositions in the home of his friend
Matthews. Then suddenly he turned completely away from
people and lived the life of a recluse, though in 1789 his *Songs
of Innocence* were published, fresh and simple poems of childhood of which the best known is "The Lamb":

> Little Lamb, who made thee?
>   Dost thou know who made thee?
> Gave thee life and bade thee feed,
> By the stream and o'er the mead;
> Gave thee clothing of delight,
> Softest clothing, woolly, bright;
> Gave thee such a tender voice
> Making all the vales rejoice?
>   Little Lamb, who made thee
>   Dost thou know who made thee?
>
> Little Lamb, I'll tell thee,
>   Little Lamb, I'll tell thee:
> He is callèd by thy name
> For he calls Himself a Lamb.
> He is meek and He is mild,
> He became a little child.
> I a child and thou a lamb,
> We are callèd by His name.

Little Lamb, God bless thee!
Little Lamb, God bless thee!

Songs of Experience was published five years later. During six years of great poverty and silence when Blake did not work but only listened to voices and visions, his wife was his greatest comfort. But when he was sixty he was rediscovered by John Linnell and other artists and during the next ten years turned out some of his finest work in illustrations. He lived to be seventy. On the very last day of his life he was singing songs of praise. Children will love the happiness, the mirth that sings in this poem from *Songs of Innocence:*

REEDS OF INNOCENCE

Piping down the valleys wild,
Piping songs of pleasant glee,
On a cloud I saw a child,
And he laughing said to me:

"Pipe a song about a lamb!"
  So I piped with merry cheer.
"Piper, pipe that song again,"
  So I piped: he wept to hear.

"Piper, sit thee down and write
  In a book that all may read."
So he vanish'd from my sight;
And I plucked a hollow reed,

And I made a rural pen,
  And I stain'd the water clear,
And I wrote my happy songs
  Every child may joy to hear.

JANE and ANN TAYLOR

Jane [1783–1824]   Ann [1782–1866]

Jane and ann taylor were two English girls who lived more than one hundred years ago and wrote verses for children. Both were born in London, a year apart, Ann in 1782, Jane in 1783. Their father soon moved to Lavenham, Suffolk, in the eastern part of England, and there they grew up. The sisters were very different. Jane, the younger one, lived in a fairy world of her own. When she was taken to the baker shop by an older brother, the baker would pick Jane up and stand her on the table where he was kneading bread. Then she would recite poems to him and tell him little stories. Her sister Ann said of her: "I can remember that Jane was always a saucy, lively entertaining little thing and the amusement and entertainment of all who knew her."

The girls' father, Isaac Taylor, was a preacher as well as an engraver and painter. He did pictures in water colors of the country near his home and made portraits of his two little girls. A picture of them hangs in the National Gallery in London. Jane and Ann were the oldest of the girls in a large family. Their house was not in the village proper but at the edge of it, so they had much space to play and romp. The two made up many of their own games and also their songs and verses in

17

the garden, and told no one about their writing. Their father was their teacher and, in spite of her large family, their mother found time for reading and writing and even published a book.

In 1796, when the girls were thirteen and fourteen, their father moved his household to Colchester to take charge of a church there. He decided that his daughters must learn a useful trade so that they might earn their own living, if the need arose. So he taught them his own trade of engraving. Every day they worked with him in the shop, helping their mother with the household tasks in the morning. Two of their brothers also worked there and would read aloud to them. Sometimes at meals their mother would be the reader, for the whole family loved books. In summer the little sisters would go for long walks together.

As Colchester was located on England's southern coast there was great fear that the French might land there, since the war with Napoleon was going on. So her parents sent Jane with the three younger children back to Lavenham and they all lived again in the old home until it was safe for them to return.

Now Jane and Ann began their life as authors. It happened one day that Ann had worked out a puzzle in rhyme and sent it to an editor. He became interested in the sisters, asked for other poems and suggested their writing some verse for children. In 1803 he published the Taylor sisters' first book, called *Original Poems for Infant Minds*. It became very popular, was reprinted in America and translated into Russian, Dutch, and German. Their second book was called *Rhymes for the Nursery*. Jane liked to write about nature and the out-of-doors. Ann liked people best. Many of her poems are stories in themselves, "Meddlesome Matty," for example.

Jane made herself a study in the attic of the Colchester house. She told her friends that the view from its windows of the sky and countryside helped her to write her poetry. At night she watched the stars. Nearly every child knows her verse, "Twinkle, twinkle, little star." It is by that verse that Jane is best remembered, as she died young. Her sister Ann married and lived to be old. Here is the complete poem that the lover of stars probably wrote as she leaned from her window:

THE STAR

Twinkle, twinkle, little star,
How I wonder what you are!
Up above the world so high,
Like a diamond in the sky.

When the blazing sun is gone,
When he nothing shines upon,
Then you show your little light
Twinkle, twinkle, all the night.

Then the traveler in the dark,
Thanks you for your tiny spark!
He could not see which way to go,
If you did not twinkle so.

In the dark blue sky you keep,
And often through my curtains peep,
For you never shut your eye
Till the sun is in the sky.

As your bright and tiny spark
Lights the traveler in the dark;
Though I know not what you are,
Twinkle, twinkle, little star.

CLEMENT CLARKE MOORE

[1779–1863]

Not many men in one short life are gifted enough to occupy five or six different positions. Yet Clement Clarke Moore was a scholar, a musician, a churchman, a poet and a professor, as well as a devoted husband and the father of six lively boys and girls. He was born in July, 1779, at Chelsea House, New York City, in the mid-year of the American Revolution. He was the only child of Benjamin Moore, a bright and serious lad, yet full of fun, and he was fortunate that his family had money enough to give him every advantage. He developed into a scholar and taught Greek and Oriental languages at the Theological Seminary near his home.

On one particular evening which was Christmas Eve, 1822, Clement Moore told his wife, Eliza, that he had a practical errand at the market. He ordered his sleigh and horses, put on his big, fur cap, top boots and warmest coat and took his coachman, Patrick, with him. Snow had fallen heavily and lay deep everywhere; roads were rough and uneven, but his horses were sure-footed and he drove them himself. He was on his way to buy a Christmas turkey large enough to satisfy the appetites of fifteen or twenty persons. Besides his wife and children and mother, he had good and faithful slaves as family servants who must be fed. Is it possible that there were two turkeys? The sleigh did not pass too many twinkling lights, as houses were few and far between in the city limits and the market lay far downtown.

But it was the blessed Christmas Eve and a feeling of pure joy surged up in Clement Moore which soon began to sing itself in musical verses. These took shape in his mind. By the time he reached the market, threw the reins to his man, and went in to select his mammoth bird, half of his poem, "The Night Before Christmas" had written itself and he could remember it. On the way home he completed the twenty-eight couplets. The hero, Santa Claus, was taken from a stout red-faced Dutchman in the neighborhood whom the author knew well.

When Clement Moore reached his house and the family sitting room, all his children—Margaret, seven; Charity, six; Benjamin, four; Mary, three; Clement, two; and Emily, eight months—on her mother's lap were waiting eagerly with their grandmother to receive him. A bright fire was blazing and all the candles were lighted. When the snow had been brushed off his clothes, their tall, slim father stood before the group and recited "The Night Before Christmas." Imagine the surprise, the merry laughs, the hand clapping before the children trooped off to bed after hanging up their stockings. Some of the little ones could hardly take in the story.

Now we all know that famous verse story which has come down to us through many generations, though the modest professor who wrote it never intended that it should have such publicity. Here are some of the lines:

" 'Twas the night before Christmas when all through the house
Not a creature was stirring, not even a mouse,

The stockings were hung by the chimney with care,
In hopes that St. Nicholas soon would be there;
The children were nestled all snug in their beds,
While visions of sugar plums danced through their heads;
And Mama in her kerchief and I in my cap,
Had just settled our brains for a long winter's nap;
When out on the lawn there arose such a clatter,
I sprang from my bed to see what was the matter.
Away to the window I flew like a flash,
Tore open the shutters and threw up the sash.
The moon, on the breast of the new-fallen snow,
Gave the luster of mid-day to objects below,
When, what to my wondering eyes should appear,
But a miniature sleigh and eight tiny reindeer,
With a little old driver so lively and quick,
I knew in a moment it must be St. Nick.
More rapid than eagles his coursers they came,
And he whistled and shouted and called them by name:
"Now Dasher! now Dancer! now Prancer and Vixen!
On Comet! on Cupid! on Donder and Blitzen!
To the top of the porch, to the top of the wall!
Now, dash away! dash away! dash away, all!"
So up to the housetops the coursers they flew,
With the sleigh full of toys and St. Nicholas, too."

Dr. Moore finally included the Christmas verses in his collected poems, but he called them simply, "A Visit from St. Nicholas." A wood engraver of Troy whose name was King gave the poem illustrations which were both quaint and delightful. They showed the steep roofs of the old Dutch houses, the pump in the middle of the street, the flying tiny reindeer, and inside of the homes, the trundle beds and nightcapped figures, who were aroused by "the prancing and pawing of each little hoof."

EDWARD LEAR

[1812–1888]

I T IS sad to think of the jovial author of the *Book of Nonsense*
as a sickly child. Yet such was the case. Edward Lear was the
youngest in a family of twenty-one children and lived in a
spacious mansion called Bowman's Lodge in Highgate, overlooking the great city of London, England. He was a cheerful,
lively small boy, though after he was seven he had attacks of
a mild form of epilepsy that he called the "Terrible Demon."
Since he was too delicate for active games with his brothers
and sisters, he spent much time in a room known as the painting room, looking at books with pictures of animals and birds.
His gifted sister Sarah gave him drawing lessons as he was
found to have a marked talent for that art. On fine afternoons
he would often be taken out to drive by his mother or older
sister Ann in one of the twelve carriages with fine horses kept
for the family's use. A footman opened the door for them, for
Edward's father was a stockbroker who had made a fortune
and gave his family every advantage. If Ann went on these
drives, she would tell her little brother the names of various
birds and flowers.

This happy life lasted until Edward was thirteen and then
everything changed with a crash. Mr. Jeremiah Lear had in-

volved himself in speculations that came to nothing and left him bankrupt. His debts were so large that he had to serve a term in prison, and his wife and children were hastily removed to London, the servants dismissed, the horses given up and Bowman's Lodge sold. The sons went abroad to seek their fortunes, the daughters went out as governesses, and only three ever married. Fortunately, the oldest sister, Ann, twenty-one years older than Edward, had been left a small income which she shared with him, and they kept house together in London. She had always been his guardian and special friend, had charge of his education and taught him at home because of his poor health.

By the time Edward Lear was fifteen he began to try his hand at sketching. The first money he earned was by making scientific charts for doctors. Then he developed an unusual skill in drawing birds, butterflies and flowers. His ability became known and presently he obtained an appointment to draw the parrots in the zoo at Regents Park. When the book containing his large colored drawings of the parrots appeared, the boy was recognized as an artist. During the next two or three years he did the plates for Dr. John Gray's book, *Tortoises, Terrapins and Turtles;* and since he drew turtles as well as he did parrots, his reputation as a draftsman of natural history subjects was made.

Lear's next adventure was with the thirteenth Earl of Derby, who was himself a naturalist and had a valuable private menagerie at his estate, Knowsley Hall, near Liverpool. Having watched Lear at work on his parrots, the Earl invited him to come down to Knowsley and make drawings of his famous collection of birds and animals. This step in young Edward's career was the beginning of a strong and long friendship.

Though he and Ann kept their rooms in London, he spent most of the next four years at Lord Derby's great house. He was then twenty, a strange, homely young man who was near-sighted, wore spectacles and stooped, had a large nose and a pasty complexion. But he possessed charm and a sense of humor. Taking his meals at first in the steward's room, he saw little of Lord Derby but became friends with his young grand-sons who found his company fascinating. Instead of sitting with their grandfather after dinner, they rushed off to visit with Lear. When the Earl inquired where they were going, they said: "Oh, to talk to that young fellow in the steward's room who is drawing the birds for you. He is so jolly!" The Earl was not offended and asked Lear to dine upstairs at his table.

The house was full of children, great-nieces and great-nephews as well as grandchildren. All, when they came to know him, adored the young artist and followed him around. There was scarcely a day when he did not pay their nurseries a visit. Entertaining in that fashionable house was quite stiff and formal, and young Lear, growing weary of it, had a long-ing to hop on one leg through the galleries! In the children's wing he could accomplish this feat. It was for the children that he began to write his nonsense limericks. The results of his work for the Earl was published years later in 1846 in a large, expensive volume entitled *The Knowsley Menagerie*, edited by Dr. Gray. But Lear's *Book of Nonsense*, with a dedi-cation to the Knowsley children, appeared at the same time. The inventive author of it never knew that in years to come his reputation would rest upon that book of humorous verse with limericks such as this, and suitable pictures to illustrate them.

There was an old man of Dembree,
Who taught little owls to drink tea;
For he said, "To eat mice is not proper or nice,"
That amiable man of Dembree.

The Knowsley episode finally ended. Lear, though an excellent craftsman, had delicate eyes, and the fine, accurate work
he had been doing strained them badly. Then he suffered from
the English climate which brought on acute attacks of bron-
chitis and asthma. He had already begun to do landscape painting, for which he had a flair, and had determined to make it
his profession. So at this time he made a decision which was
very hard on his devoted sister, Ann. He decided to go abroad
to live. She was obliged to give up their home and they never
lived together again. It seems strange that he did not take her
with him. Perhaps she did not want to go.

Lear set off for Italy in the summer of 1837 when he was
twenty-five. He went first to Florence, then to Rome which
became his headquarters for the next ten years. He found
pupils there and taught art. Living was cheap, and he did
enough lithographs for a book, *Views in Rome and Its En-
virons*. Most important of all, he met there one of the two
close friends of his life—Chichester Fortescue, a handsome
Irishman much younger than Lear and just out of Oxford.
They became friends at once, enjoying each other's society,
and their friendship lasted forty years. After another of his
books, *Illustrated Excursions in Italy*, was published, Lear went
back to England for a long visit. While he was in London,
who should hear of the clever artist but Queen Victoria! She
asked him if he would give her drawing lessons, first at Os-
borne, then at Buckingham Palace, which was an honor.
Teacher and royal pupil got on well and the Queen liked Lear.

When he returned to Rome conditions had changed and he

resolved to leave that city permanently. After traveling in Calabria, he went with a friend to Corfu, the most exquisite of the Ionian Islands. It enchanted him as Italy once had and he knew that he would return there. Meanwhile he went with friends to Athens. At Thebes the sun gave him a bad fever; but he recovered and joined his fellow travelers in Constantinople. Later on he proceeded to Egypt, and while sketching and sight-seeing there, taking in the Sphinx and the Pyramids, he bought himself "a capital hat lined with green." This may have been the "runcible hat" he described later in his verses. He found his camel easy to ride on but could make no headway with it. He said sadly: "I give my camel a bunch of green morning and evening—but all attempts at making friends are useless."

Delayed on the island of Malta by illness, he met Frank Lushington who was to become his most dearly loved friend, though he was highly reserved and Lear was not. Lushington was an English barrister younger than Lear. They spent months together making a tour of Greece while the artist sketched. His friends meant a tremendous amount to him, and those weeks were among the happiest of his life. Lear called his new friend "a diamond hidden in a tortoise's shell."

The next two years were spent in London, and it was there that Lear met Alfred Tennyson who had just been appointed poet laureate. He became devoted to this poet, his delicate charming wife, Emily, and their boys. He often stayed with them at Farringford on the Isle of Wight and played and sang (for he could sing) Tennyson's songs from *The Princess*. He was working hard at this time, holding exhibitions of his paintings in his London studio and preparing his travel books for publication. One of his pictures, "Claude Lorrain's House on the Tiber," was hung in the Royal Academy, the first of his paintings to be so honored. His summers were spent in paying visits to his friends at their various country places. Lear was always welcomed as a prized and delightful guest who was outstanding at entertaining the children.

From this time on there were no dramatic events in Lear's outward life. He was a singularly industrious painter; he had to earn his living by his work and, like all artists, his income went up and down. He was sometimes in debt and sometimes comfortably off. Then, too, he was overly generous, helping his sisters and the poor. He kept on traveling everywhere for fresh scenes to paint. He visited, he painted his pictures; he wrote the inimitable nonsense rhymes, such as:

> There was an old Man who said How
> Shall I flee from this horrible Cow?
> I will sit on the stile and continue to smile,
> Which may soften the heart of that Cow.

Inside himself Lear was often lonely, melancholy, and unhappy. As long as there were children around him he was contented and pleased. But his restless spirit drove him on to one country after another. As a result of the lucky sales of his pictures in Corfu, he made some money and engaged a manservant, an Albanian whose name was Giorgio Kokali. This man served Lear faithfully for thirty years and his master taught him to read and write. Taking tents, equipment and Giorgio with him, Lear made a tour in Palestine and resolved to see the ruins of Petra, a dangerous place to visit. "Oh, master," Giorgio cried, on seeing the colors of that Arabian valley, "we have come into a world where everything is made of chocolate, ham, curry powder and salmon!" Alas, they were attacked by Arab bandits, robbed of every cent, and nearly murdered!

Going back for a short time to Rome, Lear met the sixteen-year-old Prince of Wales, later to be Edward VII, whom he enjoyed thoroughly. But upon his next visit to England in 1860 his sister Ann, who had been in failing health, died. This was a terrific blow and left him desolate. All his life he had felt that she was his family. Ten years later his eternal wanderings ceased for a while. He had saved three thousand pounds and felt he should like to have a home of his own. So he built himself a villa at San Remo in Italy which he called the Villa Emily for Mrs. Tennyson. For a while he delighted in his house and garden. Giorgio was always with him. He had a cat named Old Foss and a bandy-legged gardener, Giuseppe. For some time they lived there in peace and quiet. Then a large hotel was built at the end of his garden, cutting off the view. Lear was wild with disgust, sold the house, and built another not far away which he named the Villa Tennyson. The new villa was to be an exact copy of the old. "Otherwise," said Lear, "Foss the cat would not like it." The Lushingtons came to stay with him and he wrote "The Pobble Who Has No Toes" to amuse their child, Gertrude, who was his god-daughter. Lear spent his last years and died in the Villa Tennyson, outliving his devoted Giorgio and the famous cat, Foss.

He had often longed to marry but never dared propose to any woman on account of his epileptic attacks. Though a lonely man, he was, all his life, most fortunate in his friends to whom he wrote literally hundreds of letters. They were very loyal, and those who were rich helped him by buying his paintings. It was a strange, weird world that Lear created of owls and pussycats, Jumblies and Yonghy-Bonghy-Bos, and the Dong with the Luminous Nose. But he was able to make it real to his readers so that they accepted it. Many of these were children who always knew what he was describing. He had an amazing mastery of rhythm and a faultless ear which caught the music of words and sound. He was a better poet than Lewis Carroll and he could invent suggestive words. No matter how absurd these words were, one recognized pictures in them. The nonsense rhymes and comic pictures were his unique and loved contribution to children's literature.

His principal books are the various journals of his wanderings; his *Nonsense Songs; More Nonsense Songs;* and *Laughable Lyrics.* In 1912 his *Complete Nonsense Book* appeared with all the original verses and pictures, together with new material selected by Lady Strachey.

While still in his prime, Lear wrote the following verses telling all about himself:

HOW PLEASANT TO KNOW MR. LEAR

"How pleasant to know Mr. Lear!"
 Who has written such volumes of stuff!
Some think him ill-tempered and queer,
 But a few think him pleasant enough.

His mind is concrete and fastidious,
 His nose is remarkably big;
His visage is more or less hideous,
 His beard it resembles a wig.

He has ears, and two eyes, and ten fingers,
 Leastways if you reckon two thumbs;
Long ago he was one of the singers,
 But now he is one of the dumbs.

He sits in a beautiful parlor,
 With hundreds of books on the wall;
He drinks a great deal of Marsala,
 But never gets tipsy at all.

He has many friends, laymen and clerical,
  Old Foss is the name of his cat;
His body is perfectly spherical,
  He weareth a runcible hat.

When he walks in a waterproof white,
  The children run after him so!
Calling out, "He's come out in his night-
  Gown, that crazy old Englishman, oh!"

He weeps by the side of the ocean,
  He weeps on the top of the hill;
He purchases pancakes and lotion
  And chocolate shrimps from the mill.

He reads but he cannot speak Spanish,
  He cannot abide ginger-beer:
Ere the days of his pilgrimage vanish,
  How pleasant to know Mr. Lear!

CHARLES KINGSLEY

[1819–1875]

*C*HARLES KINGSLEY was born on Queen Victoria's birthday, June 12, 1819. He was the eldest son of a minister, the Reverend Charles Kingsley. As a shy child he wrote poems, showed a tremendous love of nature and the sea, rocks, flowers, shells, and other sea treasures. How natural that he should write "The Three Fishers" and the *Water Babies!* When he went to school at Helston in charge of the Reverend Derwent Coleridge, he showed courage, love of truth, impatience of injustice, and a quick and deep sympathy. He progressed to Magdalen College where he took a First in classics and mathematics. At twenty-three he was sent as a curate to Eversley, and little did he dream that he would remain there for thirty-three years. Eversley was a parish in the outskirts of the old Windsor Forest. The country was wild, heathery moorland. There was a poor, uneducated population of poachers, gypsies, and "broom squires." Kingsley was young and enthusiastic and he worked hard at the parish interests which had been greatly neglected. He established a shoe club, a coal club, a loan fund, and lending library, held a school at the rectory three nights a week and Sunday School on Sunday. His constant visits to the sick and the poor, his devotion to his parish duties, his sympathetic understanding and generosity soon gained the loyal affection of all his people. Aside from parishioners, Kingsley's chief associates were officers from Sandhurst with whom he fished and rode to hounds with zest. After two years there he married Fanny Grenfell and they had four children.

Kingsley became known as a radical in spite of his deep respect for the existing social order. He advocated improved living conditions for the laboring classes, both rural and industrial, but he wanted to bring this about without political upheaval by the simple process of getting all men to live by the Golden Rule. Political events in 1848 led Kingsley into a more active part in the Christian Social movement where his ability to write was welcomed. Under this influence his first two novels were written—*Yeast, A Problem,* and *Alton Locke.* There were riots in London among the so-called Chartists. Kingsley became their champion and wrote a letter to the workingmen of England which for a time made him very unpopular. He was called the "Chartist Parson." When fever broke out in his parish he helped with the nursing and later carried on a crusade against cholera. His book, *Alton Locke,* was the supposed autobiography of a tailor who was also a poet; and to squeeze in the time for writing in his busy life Kingsley rose at five every morning and worked until breakfast. He had the gift of writing exciting boys' books like *Westward Ho,* and *Hereward the Wake,* this last a story of early Saxon England.

When he was forty he preached before the Queen and Prince Albert at Buckingham Palace and was made one of Her Majesty's chaplains. Since Prince Albert knew his record as a teacher, he asked him to give private lessons to the young Prince of Wales who had just left Oxford—and professor and pupil became real friends.

Then in 1862 Kingsley wrote the *Water Babies* for his youngest son, Grenville Arthur. His wife had protested that the older children had had books written for them and that the youngest should have his as well. The *Water Babies*, which was the story of a little chimney sweep who was changed into a sea creature, was full of charming poems, one of which is quoted below. Kingsley also brought out a book on natural science for children called *Madame How and Lady Why*. He taught his children to love nature as much as he did.

In 1856, Kingsley was made Canon of Westminster, a great honor. His arduous years of teaching, study and parish work bore fruit at last, but he did not live too long to enjoy it. He died at fifty-six.

In *Letters and Memories* it is said of him: "Charles Kingsley was as lovable in his home life as he was noble in his public life. Home was to him the most romantic thing in the world. He was like an elder brother with his four children. He built them a little house where they kept books and toys, and tea things, and where he often joined them, bringing some rare flower or insect to show them." His mother, who lived with them, once said: "I wonder if there is as much laughing in any other home in England as in ours." He loved animals, especially Dandy, his Scotch terrier, and he had two cats, a white one and a black one. On the lawn lived a family of toads who from year to year resided in the same hole in the green bank. The scythe was not allowed to come near it when the grass was cut. He had two sand wasps in a crack of the window in his dressing room. His guests were amused one day when his little girl, Rose, ran in, opened her hand, and begged him to look "at this delightful worm." A great man, a devoted parish priest, husband and father. That was Charles Kingsley.

CHARLES KINGSLEY

THE LOST DOLL

I once had a sweet little doll, dears,
　The prettiest doll in the world,
Her cheeks were so red and so white, dears,
　And her hair was so charmingly curled.
But I lost my poor little doll, dears,
　As I played on the heath one day:
And I cried for her more than a week, dears,
　But I never could find where she lay.

I found my poor little doll, dears,
　As I played on the heath one day:
Folks say she is terribly changed, dears,
　For her paint is all washed away.
And her arm trodden off by the cows, dears,
　And her hair not the least bit curled;
Yet for old sakes' sake she is still, dears,
　The prettiest doll in the world.

WILLIAM ALLINGHAM

[1824–1889]

THOSE WHO are Irish born should know the so-called "little people" intimately. The poet Allingham was no exception to the rule as he was born and spent his childhood in Ballyshannon, Donegal, Ireland, which is known as the seat of fairyland. He was the oldest child of William Allingham, a merchant and banker, and his wife, Elizabeth Crawford. Life did not lead him in the paths of dreams. His education was very brief. From a school in Ballyshannon where only Latin was taught, he was sent to a boarding school at Killeshandra, County Cavan, which he liked even less than the earlier school. He had a quick mind and an agile body and was good at sports, so it is difficult to know why at only fourteen he was put to work in his father's bank. Allingham deeply regretted the loss of schooling. But being a boy of much character, he studied and read widely and used his time so well that he mastered Greek, Latin, French and German.

In 1846, when he was twenty-two, a civil service vacancy occurred which made it possible for Allingham to leave the bank and become Principal Coast Officer of Customs. He could not devote himself entirely to writing, but he wrote in leisure hours. For many years he lived in Donegal, Ballyshannon and other Ulster towns, and it was here that he heard Irish girls singing ballads which fascinated him. He rearranged many of these songs, had them printed or sold or gave them as gifts in the neighborhood. In return for this service in the cause of popular education, Allingham, when he was forty, was given a Civil Service List pension of sixty pounds a year which was later raised to one hundred pounds.

In 1870 Allingham resigned from his position in the civil service and went to *Fraser's Magazine* as sub-editor. In 1874 he married Miss Helen Peterson, a water-color painter, and became editor of *Fraser's* until 1879.

For the sake of his wife and three small children, he went to live at Witley in Surrey, England, in 1881. Several years later they moved again to Hampstead. There a fall from a horse injured Allingham seriously and he slowly declined and died in 1889. He was great in small things such as short lyrics like "Lovely Mary Donnelly" and "The Fairies." William Butler Yeats said of him that he was the poet "of little things and little moments." He knew many of the famous authors in the literary world of his day—Carlyle, who was a real friend, Leigh Hunt, Thackeray and Tennyson, whom he visited at his home in the Isle of Wight. Besides his own poems, he published *The Ballad Book* and collections of songs, ballads and stories.

But this poet will always be remembered best by one poem, "The Fairies," which tells where the fairies lived, what they wore, what they ate and drank, their various spells. Children like it because it sings and has a dancing, tripping meter.

THE FAIRIES

Up the airy mountain,
Down the rushy glen,

37

We daren't go a-hunting
  For fear of little men;
Wee folk, good folk,
  Trooping all together;
Green jacket, red cap
  And white owl's feather!

Down along the rocky shore
  Some make their home,
They live on crispy pancakes
  Of yellow tide-foam;
Some in the reeds
  Of the black mountain lake,
With frogs for their watch-dogs,
  All night awake.

High on the hill-top
  The old King sits;
He is now so old and gray
  He's nigh lost his wits.
With a bridge of white mist
  Columbkill he crosses,
On his stately journeys
  From Slieveleague to Rosses;
Or going up with music
  On cold starry nights
To sup with the Queen
  Of the gay Northern Lights.

They stole little Bridget
  For seven years long;
When she came down again
  Her friends were all gone.
They took her lightly back,
  Between the night and morrow,
They thought that she was fast asleep,
  But she was dead with sorrow.

They have kept her ever since
   Deep within the lake,
On a bed of flag-leaves
   Watching till she wake.

By the craggy hillside,
   Through the mosses bare,
They have planted thorn-trees
   For pleasure here and there.
If any man so daring
   As dig them up in spite,
He shall find their sharpest thorns
   In his bed at night.

Up the airy mountain,
   Down the rushy glen,
We daren't go a-hunting
   For fear of little men;
Wee folk, good folk,
   Trooping all together;
Green jacket, red cap
   And white owl's feather.

CHRISTINA ROSSETTI

[1830–1894]

CHRISTINA ROSSETTI, born December 5, 1830, was a Londoner, though her father, Gabriele Rossetti, was an Italian. A scholar and poet and a revolutionary, he had fled from his native land to England and settled in London where he gave Italian lessons at King's College and translated Dante. He married Frances Polidori, herself half Italian and half English; and their four children were Maria, Dante Gabriel, Christina Georgina and William Michael.

Although this family had very little money and lived in shabby but genteel Charlotte Street in London, they had a constant stream of interesting visitors. These included Italian political refugees, scholars, writers, painters and musicians, many of them poor and struggling. Heated discussions took place to which the children listened; hatreds broke out among them. In this way the children were educated while their own talents were forming. At four years old the milkman saw little Dante Gabriel, carefully sketching his hobbyhorse. All the brothers and sisters learned verse and recited scenes from Shakespeare—and they played musical instruments as well.

The children's grandfather Polidori, a wise old man, lived thirty miles from London at Holmer Green near Great Missenden. Although his garden was small, Christina thought it a paradise, and there was a printing press kept in a shed at the bottom of the garden. Solemn little Christina with her intense hazel eyes and straight dark hair loved to take the long coach ride and visit with her grandparents at this cherished spot. She took a great interest in the small creatures she found in the garden—snails, toads, caterpillars, and spiders. Once she discovered a dead mouse which she carefully buried. Her grandfather, formerly a teacher of Italian, had retired and was interested in his printing press. When Christina was seventeen he printed her first little volume of verse on it, for he was especially fond of this granddaughter. She was a wayward child who loved to dream and to read, and among her earlier books were the *Arabian Nights* and *Melmoth the Wanderer*.

Love was to come to her early. Her brothers became members of a society called the Pre-Raphaelite Brotherhood, representing all that was fashionable in the arts. They brought out a little magazine called *The Germ*, and seven of Christina's first poems appeared in it. One of the society's members was a young painter of twenty-three, James Collinson, a stocky small youth with reddish hair. Collinson became a friend of Dante Gabriel, who liked his work. The family first saw him at Christ Church where Mrs. Rossetti and her daughters went and to which he seemed to be equally devoted. Then they missed him and found he had become a Catholic.

At this time Christina was sitting for her brother, Dante Gabriel, for an early painting he was doing, "The Girlhood of Mary, Virgin." Collinson, watching the progress of the picture, met the model. Christina was just eighteen and very pretty and he fell deeply in love with her and she with him. He told her that for her sake he would return to the Church of England—and on his doing this, she became engaged to him.

The engagement lasted several years. Then sadly enough, Collinson announced his intention of returning to the Catholic Church. So Christina broke their engagement, though she grieved deeply and from that time on became more of a mystic.

Meanwhile the next years were hard on the Rossettis. The father's health and eyesight were failing and he had to give up his teaching. William Michael, the second son, had been obliged to leave school at sixteen and go to work at the Excise Office to help support the family, while Maria took a position as governess. Christina, now twenty-one, helped her mother open a small day school. But this project was a failure, why we do not know, as Christina could be most gay and delightful with children.

After their father's death, the practical brother, William Michael, had a raise in salary and secured a house for his mother and sisters on Albany Street near Regents Park. Here Dante Gabriel, the enchanting and gifted elder brother, who was writing strikingly original poems, brought his friends. Both he and Christina had especially beautiful and musical voices, but he was witty and charming while she was shy and aloof. Among those who called at the house was a youth with large blue eyes, a rather shuffling walk, and a scholarly mind whose name was Charles Baget Cayley. He had taken lessons from the elder Rossetti and his attentive kindness to the old man won all their hearts. Next he showed that he was in love with Christina, and she encouraged him.

She had been writing poems, many of them showing sadness, disappointed love and a deep religious sense. But now she let her imagination take wing and produced a book, *Goblin Market and Other Poems*, which Macmillan published with pretty illustrations. *Goblin Market* was a rare fantasy that no young person could help liking. It was a story of two sisters, one of whom sucked deadly poison by tasting the glamorous fruits goblin merchantmen sold by the brookside in the meadow. The second sister's heroic courage saved her. Christina's descriptions of these goblins reminds us that she was fascinated by small creatures:

> One had a cat's face,
> One whisked a tail,
> One tramped at a rat's pace,
> One crawled like a snail.

In this group of poems is "The Birthday" that has lasted over the years and been set to music. The book *Goblin Market* was a success, showing all Christina's dramatic and musical talent. A few years later she published *The Prince's Progress*, a fairy tale. Her heart was ready to hope, to love again. Cayley was paying her daily visits and she enjoyed the family's circle of callers. They included noted literary men of the day— Tennyson, Browning, Ruskin, Swinburne, Gerard Manley Hopkins, and even Jenny Lind, the famous singer. This was a happy period in her life. William Michael even arranged a holiday trip on the Continent for Christina, his mother, and himself.

But after *The Prince's Progress* appeared, a crisis arose in Christina's love affair with Charles Cayley. She discovered that he was an agnostic and, as he could not change, her profound faith forbade their marriage. Besides, poor Cayley made so little money by his translations and research that he could not possibly support a wife. William Michael, who wanted his sister's happiness, generously offered to help them. But Christina's conscience would not allow her to accept such an offer from a too self-sacrificing brother. Poor Christina! Though she could not be Cayley's wife, no woman ever loved more deeply or more constantly. Cayley saw her often, brought her books, flowers and odd small gifts, one of which was a sea mouse in a bottle of spirits showing most brilliant colors. Christina showed both her humor and her delight in this present when she wrote him:

> A Venus seems my Mouse
> Come safe ashore from foaming seas
> Which in a small way and at ease
> Keeps house.
>
> An Iris seems my Mouse,
> Bright bow of that exhausted shower
> Which made a world of sweet herbs flower
> And boughs.
>
> A darling Mouse it is:—
> Part hope not likely to take wing,
> Part memory, part anything
> You please.
>
> Venus-cum-Iris Mouse,
> From shifting tides set safe apart,
> In no mere bottle, in my heart
> Keep house.

There were other animals, lively and mischievous, in which we may be sure Christina took an interest. Her brother Dante Gabriel, a widower in his thirties, had taken a house at 11 Cheyne Walk, Chelsea, that became at once a museum and a zoo. Dante Gabriel loved color. A great gorgeous peacock, displaying its plumage on the lawn, annoyed neighbors with its raucous voice. A graceful fallow deer became the next occupant. It persisted in following the peacock up and down the garden walks until it had stamped out every feather in the tail of the poor bird. Parrots and monkeys were the indoor pets. Dante Gabriel told a marvelous story of how one Sunday he was leaning back in a chair in his sitting room, listening with deep satisfaction to the musical bells from St. Luke's Church. One of the parrots who had been very surly all morning suddenly screeched at him: "You ought to be at church now." One can imagine that Christina, who was very devout, must have been horrified.

Christina's middle years came on. She was beginning in a quiet way to become famous. Oddly enough, she had barely recovered from a long illness when she brought out a book of children's verse, *Sing-Song*, one of the gayest and most delightful of all her books. Her prose and stories for children had a stilted quality, but this little volume sang and ran along like a fresh stream.

> The peacock has a score of eyes,
>   With which he cannot see;
> The codfish has a silent sound,
>   However that may be;
>
> No dandelions tell the time,
>   Although they turn to clocks:
> Cat's cradle does not hold the cat,
>   Nor foxglove fit the fox.

William Michael, after years of sacrifice for his family, married Lucy Brown, and their numerous children were a vital interest to Christina. From the first, Mary, Olive, Arthur and Helen showed that they were sprung from a literary family. They wrote plays and poems. "Christina Rossetti, A Portrait with Background" states that they "brought out a little family newspaper in which they discussed art and politics." Arthur, Christina's young nephew, the only boy, was very clever, and she once wrote him a letter which began: "My dear Arthur, I have taken an extra large sheet of paper and how it is to be filled who knews? Not I, your affectionate aunt." She does not stop there, however, but greets him on his birthday and goes on to tell the story of a kitten that carried white mice without hurting them. This episode is in "Christina Rossetti" by Margaret Sawtell. She could not help showing great partiality to these children and had nothing but praise for the efforts in short-story writing and verse-dramas that they brought for her approval.

In December of 1888 letters came from her brother's family, then in Pau, France, bringing glowing descriptions of the place and of young Olive's success in a play she herself had written in French. It had been performed at their hotel with her young brother, Arthur, taking the part of Robespierre. In Margaret Sawtell's book is quoted the letter Christina wrote in reply: "My love to my polyglot niece and the Juniors," and sent each child a letter and a present. She shared their love of pets and of nature and was homesick for them when they were abroad.

Soon after William Michael's marriage, Christina, her mother, and two aunts moved to a house at 30 Torrington Square, London, where she passed the rest of her life. She continued to write both poems and sonnets. Often they were scribbled down on scraps of paper at the edge of the washstand in her small room. Besides her poetry she cared for the older people, did household tasks, made children's scrapbooks for hospitals and was often in church. Fate decreed that with the exception of Michael she was to be the last of her family. She outlived her devoted friend, Charles Cayley, her aunts, and

her loved mother. Though admiring visitors came to call on
her and to ask questions about her work, and although her fame
mounted, many old friends were gone and she spent much
time sadly alone in the big house. William Michael was a rock
in a changing world and she left all she had to him and to his
children. After her days were done Andrew Lang wrote a
tribute to her which said: "We are now deprived of the greatest English poet of her sex which is made to inspire poetry
rather than create it." But Christina had created it. Her laurels
were won.

All children enjoy the vivid and extraordinary poem, "Goblin Market." For sheer magic it is unrivaled:

> Backwards up the mossy glen
> Turned and trooped the goblin men
> With their shrill repeated cry,
> "Come buy, come buy."
> When they reached where Laura was
> They stood stock still upon the moss,
> Leering at each other,
> Brother with queer brother;
> Signaling each other,
> Brother with sly brother.
> One set his basket down,
> One reared his plate;
> One began to weave a crown
> Of tendrils, leaves and rough nuts brown
>   (Men sell not such in any town);
> One heaved the golden weight
> Of dish and fruit to offer her:
> "Come buy, come buy," was still their cry.
> Laura stared but did not stir,
> Longed but had no money;
> The whisk-tailed merchant bade her taste
> In tones as smooth as honey,

The cat-faced purred,
The rat-paced spoke a word
Of welcome, and the snail-paced even was heard;
One parrot-voiced and jolly
Cried "Pretty Goblin" still for "Pretty Polly";—
One whistled like a bird.

But sweet-tooth Laura spoke in haste:
"Good folk, I have no coin;
To take were to purloin:
I have no copper in my purse,
I have no silver either,
And all my gold is on the furze
That shakes in windy weather
Above the rusty heather."
"You have much gold upon your head,"
They answered all together:
"Buy from us with a golden curl."
She clipped a golden precious lock,
She dropped a tear more rare than pearl. . . .

LEWIS CARROLL

[1832–1898]

Lewis carroll's real name was Charles Lutwidge Dodgson. He was the author of *Alice's Adventures in Wonderland* and *Through the Looking-Glass and What Alice Found There*, and was also a churchman, a noted mathematician and a don of Christ Church College, Oxford. In spite of all these somewhat ponderous titles, he was once a boy who had a very happy childhood.

He was born in 1832, the year of the great Reform Bill, in Daresbury, England, where his father, the Reverend Charles Dodgson had a church; and he was the eldest son and third child of eleven children. His father came of a distinguished North Country family. Although a substantial and pious person, somewhat austere, he possessed a sense of fantastic fun which his son inherited. The father was known to be an excellent classical scholar and very generous to the poor. But his income was small, his family large, so he was obliged to take pupils. Young Charles had a lovely mother. Collingwood, a nephew, said she was "one of the sweetest and gentlest women that ever lived, whom to know was to love." With good parents and a throng of brothers and sisters, life began well.

Daresbury was a secluded place. It was said that the sight of one cart passing by was an adventure to the children. Charlie, as he was called, says Derek Hudson in his *Lewis Carroll* "played in the fields, climbed trees, scrambled in and out of marl pits." Like Christina Rossetti, he was interested in little animals such as toads, snails and earthworms. In a poem, "Faces in the Fire," he says of his early days at Daresbury parsonage:

> An island-farm mid seas of corn
> Swayed by the wandering breath of morn—
> The happy spot where I was born.

When Charles was eleven his father, though greatly respected and liked by his parishioners, was appointed to the desirable Crown living of Croft in Yorkshire which boasted a larger income. The rectory was a good old-fashioned house surrounded by a garden. At its back there was also a large walled kitchen garden, and here inventive Charles was in his element. He devoted himself to entertaining the other children and made up a railway game for his brothers and sisters out of a wheelbarrow, a barrel and a small truck. Stations were arranged at intervals along the paths and precise rules laid down for crew and passengers. One of the most characteristic was: "All passengers when upset are requested to lie still until picked up, as it is requisite that at least 3 trains should go over them, to entitle them to the attention of the doctor and assistants."

Charles was the natural leader in all their games and developed a special skill in amusing little girls, as he had seven sisters. He made a box of carpenters' tools for the eldest, did conjuring tricks for them, fashioned marionettes and a theater in which he gave plays. Until he was twenty-three he worked his puppets and wrote plays for them. Canon Dodgson, the children's father, did not object to home theatricals but disapproved strongly of the regular stage.

Beneath a loose board in the floor of the nursery were stored many of Charles's youthful treasures, to be discovered years later. Among these were a thimble (Charles featured thimbles in both his fantasies), a tiny shoe and a child's white glove. Recollection may have surged up in him when he had the Alice-in-Wonderland rabbit drop his gloves. He also left an inscription on a small block of wood: "And we'll wander through the wide world and chase the buffalo." When the youthful author began to write stories, he had a special small book that he kept for sketches; and he illustrated a family magazine of which he was both editor and writer. It was called, "Useful and Instructive Poetry." One contribution was:

> Learn well your grammar,
> And never stammer,
> Write well and neatly,
> And sing most sweetly,
> Be enterprising,
> Love early rising,
> Go walk of six miles,
> Have ready quick smiles,
> Drink tea not coffee;
> Never eat toffee.
> Eat bread with butter,
> Once more, don't stutter.
> Don't waste your money,
> Abstain from honey,
> Shut doors behind you,
> (Don't slam them, mind you.)
> Drink beer, not porter.
> Don't enter the water
> Till to swim you are able.
> Sit close to the table.

Take care of a candle.
Shut the door by the handle,
Don't push with your shoulder
Until you are older.
Lose not a button.
Refuse cold mutton.
Feed your canaries.
Believe in fairies.

This magazine was followed by many others, "The Rectory," "The Comet," "The Rosebud." Charles was strongly attached to his brothers and sisters but evidently believed in good advice, especially in the matter of stuttering. Seven out of the eleven children had this affliction, including himself. At twelve his schooldays began. He had already been taught mathematics and learned a great deal at home from his father. The Richmond Grammar School, to which he was sent as a boarder, was only ten miles away. Mr. Tate, its headmaster, was impressed with young Dodgson and wrote his father: "You may fairly anticipate for him a bright career." Charles was quite contented there and sent word home to his sister that "the boys play me no tricks now." He stayed at Richmond a year and a half and always spoke of Mr. Tate as his "kind old schoolmaster." When he was fourteen he went on to Rugby and rued the day. In spite of winning many prizes he enjoyed nothing about the school where he remained for three years. Partly because he stammered he suffered from bullying. He had no knack for games of any kind and was known to play cricket only once. Being talented and sensitive, he made the best of a bad situation and worked very hard at his studies. His letters to his family were always cheerful.

He then had a delightful year at home, a golden time in preparation for Oxford. Though he was working steadily, he gave some attention to the magazine and enjoyed his charming mother and brothers and sisters. He matriculated at Christ Church, Oxford, when he was eighteen and went into residence as a commoner the next year on January 24. He had been there but two days when he was called home by his mother's sudden death. She had given him that special sympathy and interest that any writer needs and something went out of his life forever when she died. One piece of knowledge he carried away from Croft—the knowledge that he must always have children near him, that they were a necessary part of his existence. He was at this time a shy, silent young man, grateful for a friendly word. Men who sat at the table with him at meals were quite unaware of his wit and humor. Having little money, he kept very much to himself.

In November of the year he entered Oxford he won the Boulter Scholarship and at the end of 1852, when he was only twenty, obtained a First in Mathematics and a Second in Classical Moderations. After this success came another important one. He was nominated to a studentship of Christ Church (in other colleges this would have been called a fellowship) by the influence of Dr. Pusey, a friend of his father's. His father wrote to him: "You have won and well won this honor for yourself and it is bestowed as a matter of justice to you, not of kindness to me." Charles Dodgson was now a permanent student of Christ Church as long as he took Holy Orders and remained unmarried. He did remain as a student there until his death. He had one more hurdle to get over and that was the Final Mathematical School. During the summer he worked at Whitby with a reading party under Professor Bartholomew Price. After work there was time for recreation. He had been writing poems and contributed one or two to the *Whitby Gazette* under the initials "B.B." It is possible that he wrote

"The Walrus and the Carpenter" at Whitby where the beach had "quantities of sand." He had already made a reputation as a storyteller, especially with children. In October, Dodgson came out First Class in the Final Mathematical School and in December, when he was twenty-three, was given an A.B. degree.

The new collegian began to keep a diary, worked hard and well at Christ Church, was made subLibrarian a year later, and in May gained the Bostock Scholarship which added to his small income. He was now nearly independent. The famous first stanza of the "Jabberwocky" was composed about this time, put in his scrapbook and left there for seventeen years.

> 'Twas brillig and the slithy toves
> Did gyre and gimble in the wabe:
> All mimsy were the borogoves,
> And the mome raths outgrabe.

The genius of nonsense was beginning to stir. On the other hand, Dodgson was never a good lecturer but was considered dry and dull, which seems amazing. As a private tutor he did better, but as a teacher of boys (which he once attempted) he was a failure. He found them noisy and inattentive and so conceived a dislike for little boys. People found him at times very hard to understand, for there was much of the artist in him mixed up with Puritanism. He was ordained a deacon but, on account of his stammer, felt he could never be a parish priest. Yet he conducted baptisms and funerals and was even able to preach occasionally. At the time he was teaching he was asked to write for a periodical called *The Train* edited by Edmund Yates. The signed initials "B.B." did not please Yates who told him to choose a nom de plume. So Dodgson turned about the words of his name and after several experiments hit upon "Lewis Carroll," which was satisfactory.

Though fundamentally serious except with children, especially little girls, he delighted in books and the theater and eventually in photography, which became his favorite recreation. He even photographed royalty. His first book called *A Syllabus of Plane Algebraical Geometry* was published in the late 1850's and was very forbidding. On the other hand, his next book, *Rules for Court Circular*, described some special new card games he had invented. Truly this young man was an inventive genius and a very hard-working and busy person —a mathematician as well as a teller of fairy tales.

Meanwhile Dean Liddell came to Christ Church and its staid atmosphere was broken by his household and his many children. Dodgson was soon on friendly terms with Liddell's three little daughters, especially Alice, the second, who was then about five. Lorina, the eldest, was six or seven, and the third and smallest one was Edith. Their mother did not favor his friendship with the girls; still he saw them from time to time and the friendship was to develop into an "Alice" wonderland. Small Alice Liddell was most engaging and on July 4th, 1862, when he was a young man of thirty and she was ten, Dodgson and a friend, who was also a clergyman, Robinson Duckworth, took the three Liddell girls on a boating picnic three miles up the river to Godstow and its haycocks. Whenever they were with their amusing friend, there was always a great cry from the three (the Cruel Three, he called them) to "tell us a story, please." So then and there, as the boat glided along, Charles Dodgson, alias Lewis Carroll, told them the famous Alice story which he invented as he went on and called "Alice's Adventures Underground."

When the day ended and they reached the Deanery, Alice begged, "Oh, Mr. Dodgson, I wish you would write out

Alice's adventures for me." He told her he would try and sat up nearly the whole night working at the story. On August first he heard the three little girls sing a song they had learned, "Beautiful Star," and he mischievously parodied it in the song, "Beautiful Soup," which was used in the story.

In 1865, three years from the hot and sunny day of that gilded expedition, *Alice's Adventures in Wonderland*, with the John Tenniel illustrations, was published—and a special vellum-bound copy sent to young Alice. Let us hope she prized it. Her devoted friend saw less and less of her now that she had reached thirteen. In the next year his *Alice* had become a classic, taking England by storm. Old and young were fascinated by her. Soon she crossed the Channel to France and Germany, then to Italy. A Junior student of Christ Church wrote in a letter home that Mr. Dodgson, the author, who was one of his tutors, "looked something like the Hatter, a little like the Cheshire Cat, most like the Gryphon." It was rumored that the author was completely taken aback by his small book's success. No doubt as a prim and conscientious Oxford don he was. His works on mathematics were of such a different stamp and written under his own name of Dodgson. Their titles were *An Elementary Treatise on Determinants* (1867) and *Symbolic Logic* (1896).

While he was working on the second Alice book, *Through the Looking-Glass and What Alice Found There* (1871), he searched in his files for suitable poems that could be woven into the story. One was "Jabberwocky" and one was a parody (he was fond of parodies), "Upon the Lonely Moor," which became the White Knight's Song; and he drew on old nursery rhymes for "Tweedledum and Tweedledee" and "The Lion and the Unicorn." Many of these characters were in the first Alice book. The idea of the chessmen was taken from the

Liddell children who were eagerly learning to play chess. The cat Dinah was modeled on Alice Liddell's cat. When he wrote "The Hunting of the Snark" as a separate poem, its author, oddly enough, thought of the last line first when he was out walking. "For the Snark *was* a Boojum, you see"—and from that one line he pieced the rest of the poem together.

To the end of his life Charles Lutwidge Dodgson was best known as the idolized creator of the Alice books. Since he never married or had children of his own, it must have warmed his heart to know how many children loved and trusted him. One of his choicest bits of nonsense is "Alice's Recitation":

'Tis the voice of the Lobster: I heard him declare
"You have baked me too brown, I must sugar my hair."
As a duck with its eyelids, so he with his nose
Trims his belt and his buttons, and turns out his toes.

When the sands are all dry, he is gay as a lark,
And will talk in contemptuous tones of the Shark:
But, when the tide rises and sharks are around,
His voice has a timid and tremulous sound.

JAMES WHITCOMB RILEY

[1849–1916]

J AMES WHITCOMB RILEY (called "Bud" as a small boy) was
the second son of a country lawyer of Greenfield, Indiana, a
frontier town just coming into its own. When still at the mud-
pie age, Bud had the gift of remembering perfectly not only
the words people used in talking but the tone of voice in which
they were spoken. From the beginning he showed a liking for
verse. His mother, Elizabeth Marine Riley, had Welsh forebears and had once sent her own verse to local newspapers.
So this taste of her son's was probably a matter of inheritance.
When sent to a dame school, Bud was a trial to the teacher as
he had been taught to read at home and the lessons in the
primer bored him. Outside school he enjoyed himself, playing
Robin Hood up and down Brandywine Creek. His father was
very fond of this boy whom he named "James Whitcomb"
for the honored attorney who rose to be governor.

When the Greenfield Academy was started with Reuben
Riley, Bud's father, as secretary of the board, Jim, as he was
now called, was enrolled as a student. But he hated the con-
finement and discipline and continually played truant, running off to the woods and fields. He was a dreamer, an artist
in the making. Naturally there began to be an increasing gap

between his father's interests and his own. On Friday afternoons the boys in his class were supposed to recite poems they had learned. Jim had no trouble in learning "Casabianca" perfectly but was too shy to stand up and say it. Later, because he cried over a poem, "The Dying Soldier," his father whipped him. This did not better their relationship.

His acquaintance with the girl he was to dramatize as "Little Orphant Annie" came early. She was a poor spindly child who was left at the Riley house by her uncle. Her name was Mary Alice Smith. She did work for her board and keep and was always muttering and talking to herself—a real witch child. When her work was done in the evening, she told the four wondering Riley children weird tales in the kitchen or sang and danced for them. She was in the household only a few months, but Jim never forgot her.

When he was eleven the War between the States broke out. Reuben Riley enlisted for three years, becoming captain of a Union company. His older son John played in the Greenfield band to cheer the spirits of the soldiers, but Jim was too young for the band. So he bought a banjo and an aged violin; and though he never learned to read notes, he made sweet music on them, composing songs to go with the tunes. While his father was away, "Uncle Mart," who was his friend, took the Rileys in a carryall to visit an aunt who lived some miles away. The recollection of that happy visit led the boy later on to write the poem "Out to Old Aunt Mary's." But the well-loved "Granny's Come to Our House" was a tribute to a grandmother who lived near by.

Jim hated sports and loved to read, and he discovered a friend in an English immigrant named Tom Snow, who had a shoe shop but ran a circulating library as well and knew all the classics. He took note of Jim's talents and had the boy read

Dickens, his favorite, and enjoy Irving, *Don Quixote, The Swiss Family Robinson* and the *Arabian Nights*. Soon Jim had devoured all the books in Snow's library. Probably his mother had unconsciously fostered literary tastes in him. Now in his own mind he secretly resolved to become a poet. For a while his friend and schoolteacher, Lee Harris, let him edit the school paper. For this he wrote every prose item and some verse.

At last the war dragged to a close and Jim's father came home. There was now another child in the family, another one to provide for. Riley's law practice had dwindled to nothing and he was obliged to pay debts by selling their pleasant house. After that the family had to live in a succession of dingy, run-down houses. The loss of the home was a real grief to Jim who resolved that some day he would buy it back. In 1870 he should have graduated with his class, but his marks were found to be so low that the school refused to graduate him. This failure annoyed and angered his father who wished him to study law. Soon afterwards a great grief fell upon the household in the sudden death of the mother. She had always been Jim's best friend. Heartsick, he left town for a while, thinking he would sell Bibles for an agent—but found he had no talent as a salesman. When he came home, his family had moved into the old Academy building at the edge of town. He thought he would be a sign painter; and his father offered to furnish him with paint and brushes if he would go to work. Jim got as far as painting one house and hanging out his shingle, but he was still wedded to poetry and wrote it even in his paint shop. The *Greenfield Commercial* took some of his verses and he selected two poems to send his brother John in Indianapolis, "A Ballad" and "Man's Devotion," which were printed by the

Indianapolis *Mirror*. After hearing Ole Bull, the Norwegian violinist in Indianapolis, Jim had an idea of being a violinist. But though he practiced hard, he had to do some painting to keep himself out of debt.

He was twenty-three when in 1872 a patent medicine man, old whiskered "Doc" McCrillus, came in his wagon to Greenfield to dispose of his remedies. The gypsy life he led appealed to Jim Riley. Off he went with Dr. McCrillus, taking a banjo and guitar with him and becoming the entertainer of the party which included a young man of his own age, James McClanahan. Later the two traveled about the country on their own as entertainers, calling themselves "The Graphics." Jim was happier than he had been for years. Through his music and recitations he had become a romantic figure who attracted attention everywhere he went. But at times he was overcome with gloom and worry about those at home.

By this time his father must have given up all hope of his son's settling down. But Jim grew homesick, came back and agreed to study law in his father's quiet office where he could write verse undisturbed when his father was out. The law books were distasteful. At home Jim did not like the new Quaker wife and stepmother who was unkind to his sisters. But one fortunate day he composed "An Old Sweetheart of Mine," a poem that has always been popular because of its tender understanding and because every boy at some time or other is a lover:

I can see the pink sunbonnet and the little checkered dress
She wore when first I kissed her and she answered the caress
With the written declaration that, "as surely as the vine
Grew 'round the stump," she loved me—that old sweetheart of
  mine.

At this time Riley found himself to be an excellent mimic who could act the part of any character he chose. So he began to try for platform engagements. At the end of that summer of 1875, the law forgotten, this eccentric young man went off again—this time with Dr. Townsend of the Wizard Oil Company—and was a shining success. He could sing songs, draw cartoons, do impersonations. He had a pen name, "Jay Whit," but he could not place his verses and this disheartened him greatly. Then he happened to hear Robert Ingersoll speak at a meeting. Ingersoll dwelt on the importance of the common people's lives. Riley resolved to write about everyday things and sent a poem to Longfellow, asking his advice. The poet replied kindly and encouragingly. Yet all young Riley's poems continued to be rejected.

He was now nearly thirty and knew he had to find a steady job. So he took one on the *Weekly Democrat* in Indianapolis at forty dollars a month and was reporter as well as editor. But with this difference: he wrote most of his copy as well as advertisements in rhyme, and the owners of the paper apparently did not object. Meantime the citizens of Indiana were trying to develop a culture of their own and Jim Riley's sketches in verse and prose satisfied and pleased them. His lecture fee went up from five dollars to twenty-five; and Indianapolis gave him "A Complimentary Testimonial Performance" at which he was such a success that one of the judges promptly engaged him for the *Indianapolis Journal* at twenty-five dollars a week. Since he had left the *Democrat* he was glad of this offer, which gave him leave to tour the state on his lecture engagements. In that city he took a shabby little room where he wrote all his copy, both assignments and verse. Often the verse was funny, sometimes tragic.

The time came when, lecturing for the Redpath Lyceum

Bureau in Boston, he met his ideal poet Longfellow face to face. The aging poet was unable to go to the lecture so asked if Riley would read him his favorite poem, "Old-fashioned Roses." "This," said Riley, "was one of the greatest compliments I ever received."

He enjoyed writing under nom de plumes. For a long time enthusiastic readers thought that "The Ole Swimmin' Hole," "Old Worter Melon Time" and "When the Frost Is on the Punkin" were written by a farmer, Benjamin F. Johnson. Riley had invented the character of this old farmer and seemed to know him well. At last the secret leaked out and he wrote under his own name, attaining a long-sought ambition. Through the kindness of a friend who backed it, his first book, *The Ole Swimmin' Hole and 'Leven More Poems* saw the light. After this the *Century Magazine* accepted six poems and he became known locally as "The Hoosier Poet."

After the years of struggle he became a success. Mark Twain; Joel Chandler Harris, author of *Uncle Remus;* John Hay and other well-known authors wrote him letters. He lectured in cities and small towns all over the state. But he did not enjoy travel and often missed trains or took the wrong ones. One autumn at his father's house he wrote the well-known and loved verse, "Little Orphant Annie." Later he and an amusing friend, Bill Nye, took a long tour together. They never lacked good audiences. But Riley was thirty-eight before he actually made his mark. He was invited to be one of the authors to take part in a reading at Chickering Hall in New York City. James Russell Lowell was chairman of the affair and had gathered together all the famous poets of the day. The poem Riley chose to recite was "Nuthin' to Say," one of his most moving. He was very modest, this slender young man with the china blue eyes, unheralded and unknown to many. But on this occasion he had a triumph. The following year, 1888, at the Grand Opera House in New York he read "Little Orphant Annie."

After this, one book speedily followed another. When Riley made money he did what he had promised himself he would do—bought back the old family home in Greenfield, which is now a museum. He became a character in Indianapolis where he made his home with friends, Major and Mrs. Holstein of Lockerbie Street, as he never married. Once he had been in love with Ella Wheeler Wilcox, but it came to nothing. He was the devoted comrade of many children who visited him constantly and he had a host of friends of his own age as well. Success never spoiled this gentle man, who in spite of fame and admirers often doubted his own ability.

One year before the author's death, the Governor of Indiana proclaimed James Whitcomb Riley's birthday, October 7, as Riley Day. In addition to this many colleges gave him degrees, and the American Academy of Arts and Letters presented him with a gold medal. His dearest wishes were granted and good things seemed to flow to him at last like rewards in a fairy tale. When he died at sixty-seven, he was deeply mourned, not only by his own state, but by the whole country. His *Rhymes of Childhood* is his best loved book. He knew the hearts, the joys and sorrows of the people around him, big and little. No poet was more beloved in his lifetime. It does not often happen that a boy once known as an idler turns out to be a great success in the field he has chosen. Here is a verse from the favorite poem:

LITTLE ORPHANT ANNIE

Little Orphant Annie's come to our house to stay,
An' wash the cups an' saucers up and brush the crumbs away,
An' shoo the chickens off the porch, an' dust the hearth an' sweep,

WILLIAM BLAKE CLEMENT CLARKE MOORE

JANE and ANN TAYLOR

EDWARD LEAR
(*top left*)

CHARLES KINGSLEY
(*top right*)

WILLIAM ALLINGHAM
(*left*)

CHRISTINA ROSSETTI
(top left)

LEWIS CARROLL
(top right)

JAMES WHITCOMB RILEY
(right)

LAURA E. RICHARDS
(*top left*)

ROBERT LOUIS
STEVENSON (*top right*)

EUGENE FIELD
(*left*)

HILAIRE BELLOC
(*top left*)

WALTER JOHN
DE LA MARE (*top right*)

NICHOLAS VACHEL
LINDSAY (*right*)

Helen Craig

ELEANOR FARJEON
(*top left*)

ALAN ALEXANDER MILNE
(*top right*)

RACHEL LYMAN FIELD
(*left*)

STEPHEN VINCENT BENÉT
and ROSEMARY CARR
BENÉT (*top left*)

THOMAS AUGUSTINE
DALY (*top right*)

ALFRED NOYES
(*right*)

David H. Rhinelander

William A. Smith

ROBERT FROST
(*top left*)

CARL SANDBURG
(*top right*)

HENRY WADSWORTH
LONGFELLOW (*left*)

An' make the fire an' bake the bread, an' earn her board-an'-keep;
An' all us other childern when the supper things is done,
We set around the kitchen fire an' has the mostest fun
A-list'nin' to the witch-tales that Annie tells about,
An' the Gobble-uns 'at gits you
      Ef you
      Don't
       Watch
       Out!

LAURA E. RICHARDS

[1850-1943]

CHILDREN OF distinguished parents are often left a great deal to themselves while their elders pursue careers. Yet Laura Elizabeth Howe Richards, third daughter of Dr. Samuel Gridley Howe and Julia Ward Howe, shared with three sisters and a brother the most exhilarating of childhoods in which there was never a dull moment. Her father as a young man had fought with the Greeks during their war for independence. Then he became a notable pioneer in work for the blind, beginning with Laura Bridgeman (for whom the daughter Laura was named), and later was virtually the director of the Perkins Institution for the Blind in South Boston. Laura was born in Boston, probably at the Howe home, called "Green Peace," which was next door to the Institute. The children had many friends among the blind children and their teachers.

The mother, Julia Ward Howe, was not only a writer of poems and essays, most of all the renowned "Battle Hymn of the Republic," but a skilled and delightful musician who knew, as her children said, "all songs." She had a beautiful soprano voice, sang to her children in three different languages and made a special song for each of the five. She made them sing

66

with her, and in this way her daughter Laura easily absorbed ballad rhyme and meter. Though this musical mother was a student, she never neglected her children. The precious study hour that she set apart each day was frequently interrupted by a child pleading for the welfare of a sick kitten or with word of a doll's funeral. Both father and mother were the life and soul of the children's activities and conducted plays in the puppet theater, Mrs. Howe alternately grunting and squeaking the parts while her husband moved the puppets. No wonder, living as they did in a household of happy, talented grownups, that the Howe children began early to scribble stories and verse.

Laura and her brother and sisters were at first taught at home by tutors and governesses whom they often teased and tormented, for they were lively, full of mischief and often very naughty, as Mrs. Richards says in "When I Was Your Age."

In summer the whole family went to their house at Lawton's Valley, Rhode Island, six miles from Newport. Each year on the first of August the young Howes celebrated an annual festival of their own called "Yellers' Day." Gathered together on a hillside, they roared and shrieked and yelled until "they were too hoarse to make a sound." So then they rested and played something else until their voices were restored and then went at it again. They were full of imagination and nonsense. Laura and Harry, her older brother and constant companion, used to run around the dining room table playing they were animals and chanting songs they had made up. Once in an attempt to pry a lump of sugar out of the sugar barrel, Laura toppled over and was discovered with her feet sticking out of the barrel into which she had fallen head first!

When Laura had left the pranks of childhood far behind and had reached seventeen, the Cretan Insurrection broke out in

Greece. Dr. Howe felt he must go to the aid of the Greeks as he had done fifty years before. Taking his wife, Laura and Julia, their eldest girl, he set forth for Europe, spending two weeks in England en route. Here, visiting and dining with the Duke and Duchess of Argyle at Argyle Lodge, Laura saw a Highland piper in full dress enter the room and walk three times around the dining table as he played "The Campbells Are Coming."

Later, when her father had hastened on to Greece, she and her mother visited Rome. When they finally joined her father, they went to Argos and Mycenae with its Lion Gate and were actually permitted to enter the tomb of Agamemnon. Gold and jewels which were later to grace a museum were piled up at their feet. Such experiences must have left precious recollections in the mind of a young girl.

Then the greatest of romances came to Laura Howe. She fell in love with young Harry Richards whom she had met at Papini's dancing school as a child and who was to graduate in her brother Harry's class at Harvard. Both were twenty-one in 1871 when they were married, and as he was to become an architect, they took a wedding trip to Europe that he might study and learn more about his chosen profession. When they returned, they made their home for five years with Laura's parents at Green Peace where their first three children were born. Then just as the young husband was doing well, a mighty slump come in architecture; and Henry Richards' brothers, who ran the family paper mill in Gardiner, Maine, urged him to go into business with them. So the Yellow House in Gardiner became the family home and the paper mill went on bravely for a quarter of a century—then burned to the ground. In the meantime four other children had come to the Richards.

But that inventive couple opened a summer camp for boys known as "Camp Merryweather" and ran it for thirty years as a source of both income and pleasure. Their boys, to whom they were much attached, knew Laura and her husband as "Mate" and "Skipper." The camp was most popular.

In the meantime Laura on her own was providing a good part of the family income for she had become a prolific writer of children's books as well as nonsense verses. She said the rhymes "boiled and bubbled." In her early married days, whenever she needed a new hat or some other article of dress, her sister-in-law would say, "Well, Laura, write a poem and you will get ten dollars at once." Her earliest rhymes appeared in *St. Nicholas.* Now in early motherhood there came to her a great welling up of rhymes bringing their tunes with them. She says, "I wrote and sang and wrote and could not stop. My first baby, plump and placid, lay on her front across my lap. She had a broad smooth back which made an excellent writing desk."

Laura's first book, *Five Little Mice in a Mousetrap,* was published in 1880, and after several other stories, ten years later came the collection of rhymes, *In My Nursery.* This last was followed by a succession of girls' books which were easy to do as the heroines described were often her daughters and their friends through whom she heard school stories, tales of vacation and various youthful adventures. These books were most popular and one succeeded another from the pen of the head of a happy, humorous household of six children and a sympathetic husband.

Her most valuable book was her biography of her mother, *Julia Ward Howe,* which won the Pulitzer Prize. She edited also her father's letters and journals. In her house were two precious relics—her father's blunderbuss, carried by him in the Greek war, and the original copy of the "Battle Hymn of the Republic."

Many needed reforms in the town of Gardiner where she lived the rest of her life were suggested and carried out by Laura Richards. She established the high school, the library and the services of a district nurse. There was a shy, black-haired poet, a townsman of hers later to become famous— Edwin Arlington Robinson—whom she befriended and spoke of later, with great pride. She wrote sixty books; but perhaps her best-known story is "Captain January." This tale came to her when she was visiting a friend on the Maine coast, a Mrs. Door, whose house Mr. Richards had designed. From this house Laura saw a distant lighthouse, conceived an idea about it and wrote the touching little story. At first every publisher, even those in England to whom it was sent, refused it. Later it was accepted and became a best-selling book, heading the list of the author's sales. Twice it was made into a moving picture with Shirley Temple playing the part of Star.

Her nonsense jingles were so sought after that when they went out of print, they were reissued, though their author was in her eighties. They were called *Tirra Lirra; Rhymes Old and New. Tirra Lirra* was dedicated to Mrs. Richards' youngest grandson, John Richards II, and her eldest great-grandson, William Davis Ticknor III. She lived to be ninety-three and once, in her book "Stepping Westward," said joyfully of herself: "I have had a long and exceedingly happy life. May you all live as long and be as happy!"

After her nonsense rhymes appeared, she was known as the Children's American Poet Laureate of Nonsense. One of the best of them follows:

THE POOR UNFORTUNATE HOTTENTOT

A poor unfortunate Hottentot
He was not content with his lottentot;
    Quoth he, "For my dinner
    As I am a sinner,
There's nothing to put in the pottentot!"

This poor unfortunate Hottentot
Said, "Yield to starvation I'll nottentot;
    I'll see if I can't elope
    With a young antelope,—
One who would enjoy being shottentot."

This poor unfortunate Hottentot
His bow and his arrows he gottentot;
    And being stout-hearted,
    At once he departed,
And struck through the Bush at a trottentot.

This poor unfortunate Hottentot,
Was not many miles from his cottentot,
    When he chanced to set eyes on
    A snake that was pison,
A-tying itself in a knottentot.

This poor unfortunate Hottentot
Remarked, "This for me is no spottentot!
    I'd better be going
    There's really no knowing
I might on his view be a blottentot."

This poor unfortunate Hottentot,
Was turning to fly to his grottentot,
    When a lioness met him,

And suddenly ate him,
As a penny's engulfed by the slottentot.

MORAL

This poor unfortunate Hottentot
Had better have borne with his lottentot.
A simple banana
Had staved off Nirvana;
But what had become of my plottentot?

ROBERT LOUIS STEVENSON

[1850–1894]

> To where the roads on either hand
> Lead onward into fairy land,
> Where all the children dine at five,
> And all the playthings come alive.

FEW POETS, if any, have written a book for children as delightful as Stevenson's *A Child's Garden of Verses*; the vivid recollection of happy, normal childish experiences. Except in one poem, and that a cheerful one, "The Land of Counterpane," the author gives no hint of his days and years of sickness. He was the only child of Thomas Stevenson, a brilliant lighthouse engineer, and his nineteen-year-old wife, Margaret Balfour, and was born at 8 Howard Place in Edinburgh, Scotland, on November 13, 1850. His young mother had delicate lungs and he inherited this weakness from her. She had to rest in bed until noon every day throughout his childhood and could not care for him. But luckily he was in the charge of a fine Scottish nurse, Alison Cunningham, who joined the family when he was eighteen months old. He fondly called her "Cummy" and dedicated his *Child's Garden* to her who was, he said, "My second mother, my first wife, the angel of my infant life."

Louis was a high-strung nervous child, the victim of continual colds and racking coughs, whose paroxysms, combined with bad dreams, often kept him awake throughout the whole night. Cummy was his comforter, guide and friend. Sprung from Covenanting stock and a rigid Calvinist, she sometimes told such stories of the terrors of lost souls that her young charge was haunted by them. He was often regaled with exciting tales by his father who, when his boy woke crying in the night, would stand in the nursery doorway and tell of the adventures of ships, inns, old sailors and highwaymen in soothing tones, until the child drifted off to sleep again. On especially bad nights Cummy would wrap her charge in a blanket and carry him to the window, pointing to other lighted windows and assuring him that other little sick boys tended by their nurses were behind those window blinds.

Throughout the *Child's Garden of Verses* there are suggestions of his walks with Cummy and the treasures they found.

> These nuts, that I keep in the back of the nest,
> Where all my lead soldiers are lying at rest,
> Were gathered in autumn by nursie and me
> In a wood with a well by the side of the sea.
>
> This whistle we made (and how clearly it sounds!)
> By the side of a field at the end of the grounds,
> Of a branch of a plane with a knife of my own,
> It was nursie who made it, and nursie alone!

When Louis was two his father moved the family to Inverleith Terrace; but the cold and damp of this larger house resulted in continual illness for the small boy, and in a few years they moved to one with more sunshine at 17 Heriot Row. As he grew older his mother had a share in his life and became "a gay tender girl" with her son. Sometimes when the head of the house was absent at a meal, she and young Louis would enjoy dishes that the father disliked and take the top off the cream like a pair of mischievous elves.

Many story books were read to him and he early learned the beauty of words, for his Cummy was a natural narrator. Unconsciously she tuned his ear to the melody and rhythm that makes his prose musical, for she "gloated on rhythm." With the aid of a stool and a chair he preached sermons with her as his congregation. His first effort at writing was "A History of Moses" dedicated to his mother when he was six. But he did not read until he was seven or eight.

His periods of convalescence were spent at an ideal place that answered every childish wish and is described in *A Child's Garden*. It was the Manse at Colinton, his grandfather Balfour's home not far from Edinburgh. There he was put in the care of his aunt Jane Balfour, who must have seemed a ministering angel to the troop of small cousins who frequented the Manse in the summers. The house was a great roomy place overlooking the churchyard. Here ghosts or "spunkies" were sometimes known to dance. Nearby was a river with a mill wheel. In and out of the garden when he was well enough, Louis and his boy and girl cousins romped, played Red Indians or hide-and-seek. "That was my golden age," he once said. Otherwise his childhood was full of fever, nightmares, painful nights and days.

His first school at seven was near the house and no doubt his nurse escorted him there. Then he went to a preparatory school from which he often played truant when he was not ill. But now the world of books opened up. One day at Colinton he was sent to the village on an errand and carried a book of fairy tales with him. It was then "that I knew I loved reading," Stevenson says in his letters. From that time he read

Robinson Crusoe, Mayne Reid's stories and even Scott's *Rob Roy.* At eleven his parents sent him to Edinburgh Academy as a boarder, where he says he spent eighteen months of "unprofitable misery." He was lazy at lessons, would not play games and was called "a softie." So he wrote his father a letter, begging to come home. Permission was granted. Later he journeyed to the Riviera with his family. At this time Louis was so thin that "his limbs were long, lean and spidery, his chest flat and his joints made sharp corners under his clothes."

When he was fourteen and the time came for college preparation, his father entered him at the Edinburgh Seminary of a Mr. Robert Thomson, a "crammer" who only took a dozen boys. About this time he began to find comfort in comradeship; and, as he could no longer go to Colinton (his grandfather having died), he joined other boys in exploits after dark when they played tricks on the neighbors. He tells of these in *The Lantern Bearers* and says, "The words 'post-chaise,' 'the great North Road,' 'ostler' and 'nag' still sound in my ears like poetry." He never lost this taste for romance. In his school days "penny dreadfuls" became his favorite reading and his first efforts at writing followed their pattern. He compiled manuscript magazines and charged a reading fee of a penny. When he was thirteen he wrote a ghost story, a thriller, for one of these. What was more natural after that than his progression to *Treasure Island* and *Kidnapped,* as Louis was in his own way teaching himself to write. He always carried two books in his pocket, one to read and one to write in. His one wish was to express himself well and he studied masters of style and imitated Thackeray. His "crammer" succeeded in getting him into Edinburgh University the autumn when he was seventeen. Since he wore his hair long, had a gypsy-like velvet jacket, duck trousers and a loose collar, he was known to be an odd fellow and made few friends.

Meantime his father, who was devoted to him and intended him to follow the family profession, enrolled him in the engineering school, where he not only misbehaved but cut many of his classes. One teacher only, Fleeming Jenkin, who later became a real friend, Louis heartily respected. Jenkin was a young don only seventeen years older than his pupil. For nearly four years the son conformed to his father's plans for his future and spent his long vacations acquiring practical experience in engineering. The summer he was eighteen he was at Anstruther in Fife and in Wick on the bleak coast of Caithness, as pupil engineer. While at Wick he read Wilkie Collin's *The Moonstone* and studied his methods of constructing a ghost story. When twenty, he went to the Western Isles and on the steamer met Edmund Gosse, the writer, who became his friend.

In opposition to his father's Toryism, Louis became "a red-hot Socialist" and enjoyed Bohemian life with an older cousin, Bob Stevenson and two friends, Charles Baxter and James Walter Ferrier. His habits alarmed his conservative Scottish father—and when his son at twenty-one told him that he had decided not to become an engineer but a writer, Thomas Stevenson was deeply grieved and disappointed. He then insisted that his son study law that he might have a practical profession to fall back upon in case of need. But meantime young Stevenson developed lung trouble and had to be sent to Mentone in southern France. The home atmosphere colored by his father's disapproving attitude did not help him. He was gone six months and upon his return his father agreed to give him an income of eighty-four pounds a year. He was now writing essays and through a recent friend, a Mrs. Sitwell, had met Andrew Lang and Sidney Colvin, who were to prove the closest of his friends. Both these men meant much to him. Colvin urged him to send one of his original essays, "Victor Hugo's Romances," to the *Cornhill Magazine*, edited by Leslie Stephen. It was accepted but appeared signed only with the initials "R.L.S."

His father had meanwhile fallen ill, and this illness intensified his fancies about his son's behavior. He thought of him as having no morals and the wrong views on religion and politics. Yet Stevenson passed his bar examination with credit the following summer and was duly called to the Scottish bar in July 1875, when twenty-five years old. But he made no attempt to practice law. He had by this time written a number of essays and short stories and was full of enthusiasm for the career he had chosen. At this time, too, he made an important friendship that was to be of value to both him and his work. Leslie Stephen took him to the Edinburgh Infirmary to see "a poor fellow, a sort of poet who writes for him and who has been eighteen months in the Infirmary. He talked as cheerfully as if he had been in a king's palace." This man was the poet and editor, William Ernest Henley. They became great friends at once. Stevenson was impressed and touched by Henley's unquenchable courage.

Then great changes came to the author-to-be. In the spring of that year he visited Barbizon, discovered that "Henley and the Barbizonians spoke his language" and that to become an artist he must devote himself wholly to his art. Upon his return home he told his parents what for them must have been a shocking admission. For the next four years he made the journeys to France, Germany and Scotland described in *An Inland Voyage* and *Travels with a Donkey in the Cevennes*. Life out of doors improved his health. Going by way of Paris, Fontainebleau and Grez, he met at Grez the woman who became his wife, Fanny Osbourne. She was separated from her husband and living there on a pittance with her young son and daughter. They became friends and friendship deepened into love. When she was obliged to return to America to secure a divorce, he had word of her illness and followed her to California. Having little money, he went by steerage in the ship and in an emigrant train across the plains. This pilgrimage is described in *The Amateur Emigrant*, and the discomforts and hardships did his health no good. He joined Fanny Osbourne in Monterey and later in San Francisco where he fell desperately ill and she nursed him. They were married in May 1880, she being ten years older—forty to his thirty years. The doctor said Stevenson must go to the mountains at once. Since he was unable to work and Fanny had no resources, he cabled his parents for help. They decided to forgive and forget and cabled back: "Count on two hundred and fifty pounds annually." Relieved, they went on an eccentric honeymoon in the mountains north of San Francisco described in *The Silverado Squatters*. Here both Fanny and her son Lloyd contracted diphtheria, and it fell to Stevenson's lot to bring them home to San Francisco. From this time on his career is described "as a partnership of which Fanny was managing director." Stevenson's own recovery was often delayed by her various (and imagined) ailments.

When the voyage was possible they returned to Scotland that Fanny might meet his parents. But they were obliged to winter at Davos, Switzerland, for two years where he always improved but was made ill again by summers spent in Scotland. At Davos, Stevenson wrote "Thrawn Janet" and "The Body Snatcher," the former praised at once as one of his best short stories. One Christmas Day at Davos, in company with Lloyd, his stepson, a boy of eleven or twelve, he tobogganed so furiously all morning that he was exhausted and could not write. Next they went to Braemar where illness confined him to the house and he played with Lloyd's printing press and shared all the boy's games. They were fond of each other, these two, and Lloyd took the place of the son he never had. At Hyères, where they finally arrived in their wanderings, they took a charming cottage called "La Solitude." Here Stevenson spent many months which were among the happiest of his life, working four and five hours a day. Here he conceived and wrote his famous boys' book, *Treasure Island* which he sold at once to *Young Folks Magazine*. He was told by his physician that he "must live the life of a delicate girl," and later they went to Bournemouth where Henley and his wife joined them for a month. He had written four plays with Henley and was devoted to him. But his wife broke up the friendship through jealousy. His stepson, Lloyd Osbourne, said that the gaiety of Henley's visit was "the final flicker of his departing youth." In 1885 he wrote *The Strange Case of Dr. Jekyll and Mr. Hyde*, and reproached his wife for waking him from a troubled sleep. "I was dreaming such a fine bogy tale," he said. His published books increased and with them his reputation. *Kidnapped*, another boys' book, was a success. Money began to pour in.

After his father's death Stevenson had a hankering to visit the tropics and engaged a steamer *Casco* for the trip, taking all his family with him. He never again left the waters of the Pacific. After the Marquesas, Tahiti, Hawaii, he reached Samoa and there found health and vigor. He bought some land and built a house, calling it "Vailima," and became to the natives and their deposed chief (whose cause he espoused) their friend, ally and master. They called him "Tusitala," teller of tales. There in the midst of contentment and happiness he died at only forty-four, having made a high record as an author in his generation. He did not die of consumption but of apoplexy from overwork. He was buried as he wished at the top of the high peak, Vaca, carried there on the shoulders of his devoted natives, where he could lie with the sea at his feet. Boys will always remember him for the entrancing yarns like *Kidnapped, Treasure Island* and *Dr. Jekyll*. But children will find their every scene, their every recollection in *A Child's Garden of Verses*. And grownups? But we will leave them to their enjoyment of everything this master hand wrote.

GOOD AND BAD CHILDREN

Children, you are very little,
And your bones are very brittle;
If you would grow great and stately,
You must try to walk sedately.

You must still be bright and quiet,
And content with simple diet;
And remain, through all bewild'ring,
Innocent and honest children.

Happy hearts and happy faces,
Happy play in grassy places—
That was how, in ancient ages,
Children grew to kings and sages.

But the unkind and the unruly,
And the sort who eat unduly,
They must never hope for glory—
Theirs is quite a different story!

Cruel children, crying babies,
All grow up as geese and gabies,
Hated, as their age increases,
By their nephews and their nieces.

EUGENE FIELD

[1850–1895]

EUGENE AND ROSWELL FIELD, two little boys of six and five who had lost their mother, were fortunate in their transfer to the home of a young cousin who took her place. They were the children of a distinguished lawyer, Roswell Martin Field, of St. Louis, Missouri, who, driven by a busy life, had no time to care for his boys. Being desperate, he asked his sister, Mrs. Thomas Jones of Amherst, Massachusetts, if the children might come to her. As she had a young unmarried daughter at home, she consented. Her daughter, Mary Field French, was wiser than many mothers. She neither coddled her little cousins nor was rigorous with them and their first lessons were learned at her knee. The pleasant New England town with its traditions became their background and Sarah, the cook, and Jed, the hired man, their friends. Jed showed the boys what hills were good for coasting and taught Eugene how to fish. Eugene liked to linger in Sarah's spicy warm kitchen and she taught him how to set the table.

His great passion was animals. At Mrs. Ethan's shop in the village he spied the figures of the gingham dog and the calico cat who became the subjects of one of his best-loved children's poems. We are not told whether he bought them. Perhaps he did. He was busy collecting a real menagerie of live animals. First there was a dog which he washed and sprinkled with scent and named Mr. Dooley. Then there were six baby chickens that he watched over tenderly and christened Minniken and Finniken, Winniken and Dump, Boog and Poog. There were baby squirrels, too, but they escaped to their native trees. And then, oh joy, some friend gave Eugene a mole which he fed and kept snugly in his bureau drawer!

Meanwhile their father's mother, Grandma Field, began to take an interest in her grandsons and felt they ought to make her a visit. So they were sent to her home at Newfane, Vermont, some distance away, where Eugene, particularly, got into frightful mischief. His grandmother had him carry her foot warmer to church every Sunday and have it filled with coals in the vestry. Once Eugene tried writing a sermon for her and was paid ten cents for it. He wondered what she would have said if he had popped pebbles into the black velvet bag where she kept her peppermints. But he never tried that trick. The grandmother must have been a Covenanter, for she could not tolerate Christmas trees. As the children were there for Christmas they trimmed a tree—but she would not let it remain in the house and had it taken out to the village common. She called it pagan. The little boys must have been glad to go home to Amherst when Grandma had had enough of them.

When Eugene was ten, the War between the States changed life within the town and the hired man, Jed, had to go into the army. At last the fall of 1865 came and peace was declared. By that time Eugene was a tall, winning boy of fifteen with bright blue eyes and a ready smile. He was much more of an artist than a student, liked music and could recite very well. He had become a clever caricaturist and could make the most entertaining and horrifying pictures. Up to this fall he and his brother Roswell had gone to the local school. Now his grandmother persuaded their father to send them to Mr. James Tufts' Academy to board. This school was at Monson, Massachusetts, twenty-five miles away. Since Eugene did not like to study, they were to be tutored in Mr. Tufts' home; and their letters to their father were to be written in Latin that he might see for himself what their progress was!

Everything promised well. Eugene, who liked romance, seemed interested in mediaeval history and the work of Sir Thomas Malory. He even tried to write in the quaint language of Malory's *Morte d'Arthur*. Being of an inventive turn of mind, he built a moated castle in the woods behind the house, and when it was finished, Mr. Tufts was invited to come out and view his work. Unluckily, Mr. Tufts lost his balance and fell into the trench or moat. This made him angry and he shut Eugene up in his room for a whole week with no books at hand but schoolbooks. So Eugene decided to run away to Amherst. What if it was twenty-five miles! He arrived there somehow, no doubt helped by lifts in villagers' carts. But his aunt was firm. She told him (and no doubt was sorry to tell him) that what he had done was dishonorable and he would have to return and make amends. So he went back—and this act must have made a good impression on Mr. Tufts who found him very young mentally for his age. One reason was that he was rather delicate. Long suffering Mr. Tufts thought Eugene had improved and was showing some interest in his classical studies before he was supposed to enter Williams College. But his hopes were dashed when his pupil barely passed the entrance examinations. Eugene at this time, showed not the least sign of being a poet but was full of wit and fun and could declaim like a professional.

Six months went by and then Mr. Tufts received a letter from President Hopkins of Williams, saying that he did not wish to expel Eugene Field but that he would have to be withdrawn from the class. The boy, now eighteen, had become a nuisance. He would not work but spent his time boxing and writing satires on the faculty. So Williams College passed from his ken. And then came sad news from St. Louis of the death of the boys' father. This was a genuine sorrow to both of them.

Mr. Field had provided two guardians for his sons, since they were minors. One of these men, John William Burgess, was young himself, only twenty-five. The guardians agreed that Eugene should enter Knox College at Galesburg, Illinois, as a sophomore. Burgess was a teacher there and could keep an eye on him. This plan was unsuccessful. Rascally Eugene had come into some money which he spent like water, living in a hotel room where he could entertain his friends. When he did not win the prize for declamation, he tied a calf to the bell rope of one of the college halls so that the bell pealed furiously all night. When Livy, a Latin author hated by the students, was burned in effigy, Eugene was known to have had a hand in it, and the college nearly caught fire. Going home with a girl he liked, Eugene incurred the father's wrath and had a pitcher of cold water thrown over him! He finally had to leave Knox and go to the University of Missouri where his brother Roswell was studying. The results of this change were much the same, though he did begin to write verse and edited a paper of his own called the *University Missourian.*

A new and good friend, Edgar Comstock, took Eugene to his home in St. Joseph for a visit. There Eugene's eyes fell upon a most attractive girl of sixteen, Edgar's sister, Julia. "I shall marry her," he declared. But on approaching Julia's father, he was told that he must wait four years until he had a suitable job and could support a wife. Eugene was in love and wished to marry immediately. He thought he could act and obtained an interview with the great Shakespearean actor, Edwin Forrest. When Forrest had heard him recite, he said coldly, "Go back to your friends and tell them to apprentice you to a wood sawyer!"

This was discouraging. As he had eight thousand dollars of his own, the lover decided to go abroad with Edgar. Through his extravagance the money was soon exhausted and Mr. Melville Gray, his other guardian, notified Eugene of this sad fact. He was mortified by having to sell the expensive presents he was bringing home in order to get home himself. Now he found himself penniless. His only firm resolve was to make Julia Comstock his wife. Through a friend he was given an interview by Mr. Hutchins, editor of the *St. Louis Journal*. "Well," said the editor, "you can write me a review of *Romeo and Juliet*, now running at the Olympia Theater."

Eugene put his best efforts into this review and, though it was ruthlessly shortened, it led to a job. He married his Julia —and wonder of wonders, was soon promoted to be city editor on the *Journal*. His articles were full of humor and began to attract attention. He was offered the city editorship of the *St. Joseph Gazette*, which meant more money.

It was singular that this young man who had never been a student, now became a desperately hard worker. In his leisure moments he wrote rhymes, the most popular being his famous "Little Peach." It became a universal favorite and was reprinted, translated and made into a song. Eugene was also found to be a valuable man for news. He wrote up the Custer Massacre and got a "scoop" for the paper. Shortly after this he returned to St. Louis to be on the *Journal* and *Times-Journal*.

He was now a columnist and called his column "Funny Fancies," into which he put everything that amused or impressed him in his daily life. Gay by nature, he wished to amuse others. Yet occasionally he could be deadly serious as in the poem "Christmas Treasures."

His family increased in size; he had to have a larger salary. So he moved to Kansas City as editor of the *Times* with his brother Roswell. A better opportunity came. He was offered the managing editorship of the *Denver Tribune* and went to Denver, a lawless city at that time. Its citizens wanted an honest editor and Eugene Field was known to be both honest and fearless. While there he wrote his rhymes for the *Tribune Primer*—outrageous but most amusing. Long before this Julia had undertaken the management of his salary. The family had to be kept going, and Eugene on his way home was apt to spend half of it on some expensive article or give his overcoat to a beggar. He was a natural spendthrift though a devoted husband and father. He called his many children by all manner of nicknames, "Trotty," "Daisy," "Pinney."

He had been in Denver three years and was thirty-three when Mr. Stone of Chicago, who published the *Chicago Daily News*, came to Denver and promptly engaged Field as columnist. So the Field family moved to Chicago. The new column was called "Sharps and Flats." It did not become popular at once, but when it did, it was watched for eagerly by every reader of the paper. It covered politics, baseball, music, notes on the theater. Eugene, who had never outgrown his love of pranks, wrote in his office in a burlap garment with carpet slippers on his feet and a skull cap on his head. He enjoyed company and practical jokes. Once he wrote Mr. Stone to send him a suit of clothes instead of a turkey for Thanksgiving. Mr. Stone was equal to him and sent the turkey as usual and with it a convict's striped suit from the penitentiary. But he did not count on his young columnist's wearing it to the office—which he often did, telling visitors he was a "trusty" on parole. Poor Mr. Stone!

Eugene's first book was *The Denver Tribune Primer* and it was most popular. Then he wrote a poem called "Little Boy Blue" which sold like wildfire. He was amazed at its success. Of course it soon found a place in one of his later books, *Poems of Childhood*. He was now in a secure position and did not have to go to the office every day. His son fetched and carried his copy, and Eugene began to study the classics that he had so sedulously neglected in his youth. He found languages easy, mastered Latin and wrote amusing satires on the odes of Horace. *A Little Book of Profitable Tales* and *A Little Book of Western Verse* soon made their appearance. But their author, worn out, was near a nervous breakdown and the doctor advised him to take a trip to Europe. So he and Julia, with all their family, decided to take an ocean voyage. They left the children in a good school in Hanover, Germany, while they traveled about Europe. Little did they dream of tragedy when it fell suddenly upon them. Their oldest boy caught some unknown infection and died suddenly. This blow was too much for Eugene and, homesick as well, he curtailed their time abroad and they sailed for home. His health had not benefited and he was heartbroken.

Now he developed into a remarkable lecturer and public reader because of his rich, musical voice which appealed to every audience. But this was exhausting work and Julia begged him to give it up since his books were selling splendidly. Soon he had money enough to buy a home which they named the Sabine Farm in Buena Park, a suburb of Chicago. Eugene loved it but lived only two months to enjoy it.

"Gene" Field, as all his devoted friends and admirers called him, was universally mourned. All children loved him, and many of his verses like "Wynken, Blynken and Nod," "The Dinkey-Bird," "Little Boy Blue," "The Sugar-Plum Tree" and "Seein' Things" became nursery classics. His big heart responded to any case of need and he endeavored to relieve it. He realized that most human beings need more laughter in their lives and he was one of the people who could give it to them. This was a great gift and one for which he was long remembered. The tenderly pathetic mingled with the humorous in his children's poems. One of the best and most lively is "The Duel":

THE DUEL

The gingham dog and the calico cat
Side by side on the table sat;
'Twas half past twelve and (what do you think!)
Nor one nor t'other had slept a wink!
　The old Dutch clock and the Chinese plate
　Appeared to know as sure as fate
There was going to be a terrible spat,
　　(*I wasn't there; I simply state*
　　What was told to me by the Chinese plate!)

The gingham dog went "Bow-wow-wow!"
And the calico cat replied "Mee-ow!"
The air was littered, an hour or so,
With bits of gingham and calico,
　While the old Dutch clock in the chimney place
　Up with its hands before its face,
For it always dreaded a family row!
　　(*Now mind: I'm only telling you*
　　What the old Dutch clock declares is true!)

The Chinese plate looked very blue,
And wailed, "Oh dear! what shall we do!"
But the gingham dog and the calico cat
Wallowed this way and tumbled that,
  Employing every tooth and claw
  In the awfullest way you ever saw
And oh! how the gingham and calico flew!
    (Don't fancy I exaggerate—
    I got my news from the Chinese plate!)

Next morning where the two had sat
They found no trace of dog or cat!
And some folks think unto this day
That burglars stole that pair away!
  But the truth about the cat and pup
  Is this: they ate each other up!
Now what do you really think of that!
    (The old Dutch clock it told me so,
    And that is how I came to know.)

HILAIRE BELLOC

[1870–1953]

I<small>T</small> <small>IS</small> remarkable that Hilaire Belloc, one of the most versatile and distinguished Englishmen of letters of his time, took such immense pleasure in writing for children. Those who know *The Bad Child's Book of Beasts* and *Nine Cautionary Tales and a Moral,* written early in his career, can imagine the chuckles that must have accompanied his work on these beasts and the laughter of the children and young people who read them.

The author (christened Joseph Hilaire Pierre Belloc) was born in France in 1870, which was the beginning of the Franco-Prussian War. He was the son of Louis Belloc, a French barrister, and his English wife, Bessie Raynor Parkes. He lost his father when two years old. After a happy childhood spent between France and England with his mother and sister, he entered the Oratory School, Birmingham, England, at ten years old, as his family were Catholics. Speaight's life of him says, he was "acutely miserable at first but later fitted in." The Oratory was no worse than other public schools. He was known as a small, self-possessed, calm, detached lad who won English and debating prizes and was a success on the school stage. Later on he took no interest in the theater. He read

Tom Sawyer, Huckleberry Finn, Glaiser's *Travels in the Air* and *Masterman Ready.* He declares that Church's *Stories from Homer* "illuminated my life from my tenth to my twentieth year." As yet he gave no sign of genius or marked originality. Two intimate friends, Charles Somers Cooks and Arthur Pollen, were made at this school, which he left at seventeen. Then came his military service and he was for a year or so with the 8th Regiment of French artillery at Toul and Meurthe-et-Moselle, as a driver.

In 1893 he went up to Balliol College, Oxford, where he read history, one of his favorite subjects, and became president of the Union (the University Debating Society). He won the Brackenbury Historical Scholarship and was graduated with first-class honors in 1895 after an amazingly short period of study. As soon as college was over he began to write and gained considerable repute from magazines and newspapers. At the same time he began his career as an author. *Verses and Sonnets,* the first of his lengthy list of books, was his earliest published volume in 1895, and a year later came *The Bad Child's Book of Beasts.* Meanwhile he had met Elodie Hogan, an American girl, in Rome while serving with the army and had determined to make her his wife. She shared his religion and they were married in 1896. He had hoped to obtain a full fellowship, and as he had been virtually promised one, he took a house in Oxford. The fellowship was given to someone else and he had to write books, give lectures and take pupils to support himself, his wife and baby. His family grew steadily until he had five children.

Meanwhile in 1899 his biography of Danton appeared and that of Robespierre two years later. Both were compelling and lively books. But his best-loved work was *The Path to Rome.* In it Belloc describes a walk from his old garrison town

of Toul, France, to the Eternal City. The book is full of
humor, staunch Catholicism and the love of traveling that
shone through all his work. About this time Gilbert Keith
Chesterton became a devoted friend of Belloc's, sharing many
of his views, 'his love of the mediaeval period, his opposition
to socialism and his political opinions.' These two men with
Cecil Chesterton, Gilbert's brother, founded a weekly paper
called *The Eye Witness*. Bernard Shaw, another friend, called
it the "Chesterbelloc."

In 1906 the Bellocs bought a place in Sussex that Elodie
Belloc describes as "a lovely long brick house." This was
"King's Land," which was to be Belloc's home for the rest of
his life. They had bought it with five acres and a mill attached
for one thousand pounds. They needed the room it afforded.

It was said of this loved house that was such a joy to each
and every member of his family that: "To walk through the
rooms of 'King's Land' was to make a journey into the past.
The pictures, the statues, the furniture, the books, even the
hundred and one things he had picked up on his travels or
been given by friends or his children, were treasured land-
marks in his life and the lives of his forebears. For years a toy
stork, suspended on a wire from the ceiling, which had been
given to him by his daughter, used to swing to and fro as the
door of the room opened. This became a tradition and stories
collected round it."

Belloc had strong superstitions. Certain herbs and blossoms
could never be brought into the house, and this list included
the glorious golden wild broom which he considered highly
unlucky.

From his famous essay, *A Remaining Christmas*, a description of the celebration of Christmas Eve at King's Land should
be quoted here because of the beauty of its religious spirit,

overflowing hospitality and joy in children:

"The holly and greenery were brought from a neighboring wood, and the house was decorated with these just before dark on Christmas Eve. Then there is brought into the hall a young pine tree about twice the height of a man, to serve for a Christmas tree, and on this innumerable little candles are fixed, and presents for all the household and the guests and the children of the village. It is at about five o'clock that these last come into the house, and at that hour in England, at that date, it has long been quite dark; so they come into a house all illuminated with the Christmas tree shining like a cluster of many stars seen through a glass.

"The first thing done after the entry of these people from the village and their children (the children are in number about fifty—for this remote place does not shrink or grow but remains itself) is a common meal, where all eat and drink their fill in the offices. Then the children come in to the Christmas tree. They are each given a silver piece one by one and, one by one, their presents. After that they dance in the hall and sing songs, which have been handed down to them for one does not know how long. These songs are game-songs and are sung to keep time with the various parts in each game, and the men and things and animals which you hear mentioned in these songs are all of that countryside. Indeed the tradition of Christmas here is what it should be everywhere, knit into the very stuff of the place; so that the little children, when they think of Bethlehem, see it in their minds as though it were in the winter depth of England. . . . These games and songs continue for as long as they will and then the children file out past the great fire in the hearth to a small place adjoining where a crib has been set up with images of Our Lady and Saint Joseph, the Holy Child, the shepherds and what I will

94

call the Holy Animals. And here again tradition is so strong in this house that these figures are never new-bought but are as old as the oldest of the children of the family, now with children of their own. On this account the donkey has lost one of its plaster ears and the old ox which used to be all brown is now piebald, and of the shepherds, one actually has no head. But all that is lacking is imagined. There hangs from the roof of the crib over the Holy Child a tinsel star, grown rather obscure after all these years and much too large for the place. Before this crib the children sing their carols . . . There are half a dozen or so of these carols which the children here sing, and mixed with their voices is the voice of the miller . . . The miller is famous in these parts for his singing, having a very deep and loud voice which is his pride. When these carols are over, all disperse, except those who are living in the house, but the older ones are not allowed to go without more hot drink—a sustenance for Christian men."

Belloc's historical writing includes a *General Sketch of the European War*, a four-volume history of England and a study of the Jews. Intense Catholic feeling colors all his historical thought. But he wrote light novels, too, and the travel he loved inspired much of his work. His sense of the past was deep and he warmed to enthusiastic praise over his native Sussex. But what he will be remembered for is his "uniquely individual handling of our language springing from an immense zest for life." Work for hours and hours together was for him "a consuming fire."

A few months before the breaking out of the Great War the great sorrow of his life fell upon Belloc. His cherished wife died after a short illness, leaving him with a growing family of sons and daughters. Though he was to do much work in the future and outlive her for many years, he was never the same man again. But his books continued to be written and he gained a great reputation in the land he loved, regarded as a foremost man of letters. He had a host of loyal and devoted friends. His son-in-law Reginald Jebb said of him in Speaight's *Life:* "With children Belloc was unusually popular. He fascinated them by doing surprising and delectable things, such as carrying them off at bedtime in their dressing gowns to look at the moon through a big telescope, or making realistic birds out of paper that flapped their wings when you pulled their tails . . . Though he could be a stern parent . . . in his heart Belloc idealized children and wrote of them and to them with deep feeling. That he understood what would amuse them is borne out by the perennial popularity of the *Cautionary Tales.* In appearance this giant of entertainers was massive and stocky, with a strong jaw and a square head."

Hilaire Belloc's last years were made happy by the presence of his elder daughter, Eleanor, who with her husband, Reginald Jebb, and their four children came to live with him at King's Land. His son-in-law ran the farm and Eleanor, his house. The children were a constant delight. They must have been pleased with "Henry King," the *Cautionary* verse quoted below.

HENRY KING

The Chief Defect of Henry King
Was chewing little bits of String.
At last he swallowed some which tied
Itself in ugly knots inside.
Physicians of the Utmost Fame
Were called at once; but when they came
They answered, as they took their Fees,
"There is no cure for this Disease.

96

Henry will very soon be dead."
His Parents stood about his Bed
Lamenting his Untimely Death,
When Henry, with his Latest Breath,
Cried, "Oh, my Friends, be warned by me,
That Breakfast, Dinner, Lunch and Tea
Are all the Human Frame requires . . ."
With that, the Wretched Child expires.

And as a final admonishment its author might have added to
some grandchild inclined to carelessness:

Child! do not throw this book about;
Refrain from the unholy pleasure
Of cutting all the pictures out!

WALTER JOHN DE LA MARE

[1873-1956]

WALTER JOHN DE LA MARE, the English poet who for many years charmed children by his easy entrance into the world of their imagination, was born in the village of Charlton in Kent. His father, whom he lost in childhood, James Edward de la Mare, was a churchwarden and brother to the Reverend Abraham de la Mare, rector of St. Thomas's, Woolwich; and his mother was Lucy Sophia, daughter of Dr. Colin Arrot Browning, naval surgeon, Woolwich Dockyard. Dr. Browning was an unusual man who completed his career as a naval surgeon by reforming the method of treating the wretched people on the convict ships bound for Australia. In 1842 he published a book, *English Exiles*, and the next year a second one, *The Convict Ship*. By means of these, his sermons and his scriptural lessons, the good and humane old surgeon was finally able to dispense with the system of keeping the convicts in irons—and to give them freedom of movement on board ship.

De la Mare's father was of Huguenot descent and it has been fairly well established that this poet is related on his mother's side to Robert Browning through a second marriage of Browning's grandfather. The stream of poetry ran in him from the beginning. Since the boy De la Mare and his mother were close companions, he shared his early efforts at verse with her and pays her a touching tribute in his poem, "To My Mother."

At sixteen, Walter de la Mare was sent to St. Paul's School in London's great cathedral, noted for its boys' choir. Since he sang in the choir, young De la Mare called the school magazine he founded *The Choristers' Journal*. He not only edited but probably wrote most of the nine issues. Among the advertisements there were veiled suggestions for certain stamps as he had a cherished stamp collection. In fact, Chesterton once said of him that he gathered together "tiny objects hardly to be seen with the naked eye" as a hobby. The advertisement ran:

Stamps, Stamps, Stamps!
Keep your money till De la Mare gets his superb
duplicate collection.

The title page of No. 1 of *The Choristers' Journal* contained the following suggestions to contributors:

"The paper will be published every Tuesday at 5 P.M. and all Correspondence must be sent in before 6 P.M. on Fridays, and must be put in the first shelf of the cupboard under No. 2 Locker, and must be marked in the right hand corner whether Joke, Question, etc., and be signed with full name and then either initials or noms de plume beneath."

Among other contributions De la Mare wrote two stories for the magazine, "Powder Monkey Bob" and "A Moonlight Skate," the latter a vivid piece of description of a stay at a Russian château. He was already trying his poetic and literary wings. He had a good voice; but when it broke suddenly and

99

disastrously in the midst of an important piece of music given by the choir, the choirmaster was able by a swift signal to keep him from further singing for fear of straining it. He left St. Paul's in 1890 when not yet eighteen, as it was necessary for him to go to work.

Though he might have chosen banking, he chose the Anglo-American (Standard) Oil Company and became a book-keeper in the statistical department. But since he had begun to think of himself as a poet, he kept his hair long and wavy in the style of the French Latin Quarter and wore a velvet coat which must have amused his fellow workers. However, he was allowed to edit and write a house organ which reached two issues. His first novel (1904) was written on scraps of the firm's paper. What a dull world was the one in which this gifted young man passed his days! It is certain he must have done his work with ability and accuracy since he remained with the firm eighteen years until he was thirty-five. But he had to have some interest as a compensation for the dullness, and "to keep his spirit alive," he turned to fantasy.

The Sketch finally published "Kismet," a short story which was his first paid appearance in print. A couple of years later he sold another story, "A Mote," to the *Cornhill Magazine* and followed it by "The Village of Old Age," a fantasy. Both these last were good but not of the same high quality as "The Moon's Miracle," which appeared in a later number of the *Cornhill*. De la Mare was always happy in his descriptions of the moon and her own especial enchantment. In "Silver" he does this to perfection:

> Slowly, silently, now the moon
> Walks the night in her silver shoon;
> This way, and that, she peers, and sees

Silver fruit upon silver trees;
One by one the casements catch
Her beams beneath the silvery thatch;
Couched in his kennel, like a log,
With paws of silver sleeps the dog;
From their shadowy cote the white breasts peep
Of doves in a silver-feathered sleep;
A harvest mouse goes scampering by,
With silver claws and silver eye;
And moveless fish in the water gleam,
By silver reeds in a silver stream.

During these years and at the time of the publication of his first book, *Songs of Childhood*, in 1902, De la Mare did not sign his own name but called himself "Walter Ramal."

In 1908 the Asquith Government became aware of his great talent, and on Sir Henry Newbolt's recommendation De la Mare was given a small grant and placed on a Civil List pension of a hundred pounds yearly. He was then able to leave the Anglo-American Oil Company permanently. But he was now a husband and the father of four children and had to supplement his income by free-lance work and much book reviewing for which, while he did it well, he never cared. However, after a second collection of poems and another novel, *Memoirs of a Midget* (1921), which won the James Tait Black prize, he obtained enough security to retire to the country and write his books. His most important novel was *The Memoirs of a Midget*, a remarkable conceived story of a woman who was just like all other mortals except in miniature. There is a story that De la Mare created the *Midget* because his children came home one day full of enthusiasm over a midget they had seen at a circus or some entertainment. "I shall write about a midget," their father announced. And he did.

Though a novelist, Walter de la Mare was first and foremost a poet, dwelling as no other writer has done in the same way on a shadowy border line between the real and the unreal. Even in his poems written especially for children, like the inimitable *Peacock Pie* and *Bells and Grass*, one is aware of a mysterious country, delightsome to enter. In his later years this poet attained the honors and distinction he so richly deserved. He was one of the twenty-four persons to be given the Order of Merit. Four universities made him a doctor of letters; he was an honorary Fellow of Keble College, Oxford, and also an honorary Fellow of the American Academy of Arts and Letters. For half a century he continued to produce his work, until he was eighty-three. Book followed book as the years went forward: *The Return, Peacock Pie, Collected Poems;* fantasies, *The Three Royal Monkeys* and *Lord Fish;* his anthologies, *Come Hither, Early in the Morning, Love, Behold This Dreamer;* and in 1949, his *Collected Tales* and the height of his poetry in *The Burning Glass* and *Winged Chariot.*

As a person De la Mare was one not to be forgotten—a gentle, wise and hospitable being, possessed of great charm and humor and, despite the depths of his philosophy, comprehending perfectly the world of childhood's imagination. He had, as someone said, "a dark Roman profile," and an air of mystery seemed to envelope him. "He worked in a farther land darkly unknown to us, but of which he had astonishing intimations." In his introduction to *Bells and Grass,* he said: "I know that only the rarest kind of best in anything can be good enough for the young." Here is one of his amusing poems about something that happens to us every day as it happened to "Miss T."

MISS T.

It's a very odd thing—
   As odd as can be—
That whatever Miss T. eats
   Turns into Miss T.
Porridge and apples,
   Mince, muffins and mutton,
Jam, junket, jumbles—
   Not a rap, not a button
It matters; the moment
   They're out of her plate,
Though shared by Miss Butcher
   And sour Mr. Bate;
Tiny and cheerful,
   And neat as can be,
Whatever Miss T. eats
   Turns into Miss T.

NICHOLAS VACHEL LINDSAY

[1879–1931]

NICHOLAS VACHEL LINDSAY was born on November 10th, in Springfield, Illinois, the town of the Middle West made notable by the great man Abraham Lincoln. The very house on South Fifth Street in which the poet came into the world had belonged to one of Mary Todd Lincoln's sisters, and Lincoln, when a lawyer, had visited there and actually slept in the room of Vachel's birth. The Illinois Executive Mansion was next door. What wonder that Lincoln became one of Vachel's heroes!

The boy's father, Dr. Vachel Thomas Lindsay, was a powerful man, an old-fashioned country doctor, conscientious and beloved by the ordinary people of the town. With his mother, Esther Frazee Lindsay, there was a different and closer relationship. As a girl, she had written verse and been an art student; she still lectured on European artists and organized pageants. In one of these, called *Olympus*, Vachel, with yellow curls, played the part of Cupid. Though a club woman his mother worked zealously for missionary societies, and both parents were devoted members of the Campbellite or First Christian Church that Vachel joined when he was eleven. His mother had many strains in her inheritance, Scotch, English,

Welsh, Spanish and Indian. He wrote of her: "My Mama is unquestionably the most powerful personality I have ever known."

Vachel had a sister Olive, two years older and very close to him, and a much younger sister, Joy. As a child he was frail, having had a desperate illness as a baby. He was kept out of school, his mother teaching him at home. Before he knew his letters he remembered his father's reading of *Uncle Remus* and his parents and sister Olive taking turns at reading Scott aloud under the lamp. When at last he himself could read he began with *Grimm's Fairy Tales* and delighted in them, progressing to *Tom Sawyer*, *Huckleberry Finn*, Poe's poems and a ponderous two-volume Rawlinson's *History of Egypt* given him by his father. He went on from there to *A History of Japanese Monosyllables*, Stanley's *Darkest Africa*, Dante—and most of all, *Paradise Lost*. He said it was Milton who made him a poet at nine years of age.

His biography "West-going Heart" by Eleanor Ruggles states that Vachel was not shy but "an affectionate and excitable little boy who raced up and down Fifth Street wearing his Indian suit, a big kite tugging at his arm." When their parents were away, he and Olive played their favorite game with Lucy, the cook, a tall, powerful and very black woman. With her kinky hair streaming and stuck through with feathers, she would lead the children in single file around and around the outside of the house while all three chanted in a transport, "Injun chief! Injun chief! Injun chief!"

When stronger he was sent to Stuart Grammar School and won two essay prizes, one on *Labor and Learning* and one for *Advantages of Farm and City Life*. At fourteen he went to Springfield High School and there made a warm friend in a teacher, Miss Susan Wilcox, who was interested in poetry, taught English, botany and zoology. He was very lucky in his adolescence to have found such an understanding teacher. "You might have made a scientist of me," he suggested one day. She shook her head. "Not in a thousand years."

Vachel and another boy once played with matches, setting fire to a farmer's barns. For this Dr. Lindsay gave his son a good flogging that he never forgot and never forgave. His father became an admirable but terrible figure to him. The doctor, planning that his son should follow in his footsteps, later gave him a box of jumbled bones from an old skeleton and said, "Learn to put these together." The boy tried but could not succeed. Only their shapes interested him and so he found pleasure in sketching them. When he had to put up his father's big horse in the stable, he was always terrified; but he used to chant Tennyson's poem, "Maud," whose martial rhythm cheered him while he unharnessed and bedded the horse.

One of Vachel's pleasures beside the nickelodeons and the ice-cream parlor was to loiter about the Leland Hotel, to talk with the waiters in the huge room where they chopped wood. He drank in their tales, their songs and music. When he was ready for college and Susan Wilcox asked him about his plans for the future, he answered: "If I were an orphan I'd be an artist. But I'm not and so I'm going to college and be a doctor."

Olive had been kept at home a year so that her brother could catch up with her, and in 1897 the two entered Hiram Christian College at Hiram, Ohio, together, Vachel with the full intention of studying medicine and doing what his parents wished. But though he tried, he was never interested in the medical courses and enjoyed his college life in other ways, one of which was helping to illustrate the college annuals. He read widely at this time, finding pleasure in Emerson, Lowell,

Poe, Ruskin and Kipling. He was a young man full of ideals, with a profound and simple faith, and his great desire was to devote himself to the service of his fellow men. This idea haunted him. When he was twenty he wrote his parents a revolutionary letter, saying that he was giving up his medical education and going to study art. Both parents were willing to help. But his mother wrote "that his father feared he was giving up the certainty of a useful vocation for a very uncertain dream." His father was not in good health nor was his work bringing in much money. Vachel resolved to ask for as little money as possible.

So he left college, going in 1900 to the Art Institute in Chicago where he spent much time in the Field Museum. Often he had only a dime for a meal and breakfast would be cream puffs, lunch an oyster sandwich, and supper a bag of cookies or chocolate almonds. Before Christmas he got a position in the toy department of Marshal Field's store, but the grueling Christmas rush when the boys worked from eight-thirty to midnight exhausted him and he went home. His next Mecca was New York in 1904 where he studied with Robert Henri who was teaching in the Chase Art School. He had his parents' consent for this venture, but it was hard on them financially. Although he admired Henri and they became friends, he never drew particularly well. "I am on the bum," he wrote in his diary, and to his father, "Two things are settled with me. First that I shall pay my way and secondly I shall live and die an artist." Meanwhile eventually he had to go home to live. *McClure's, The Bookman, Everybody's Magazine* and *The Century* had all refused every one of the poems and drawings he had submitted! When his sister married his college friend, Paul Wakeman, he gave her two of his poems as a wedding present. "Always understanding" in the matter

of his poetry, he said of her, just as his father without understanding of what he was aiming at, had stood by him, financially.

At long last, when Vachel was twenty-five, had been in and
out of love twice and broken one engagement, the *New York
Critic* published his poem, "The Queen of Bubbles." Now he
felt he must earn his own living. Back in New York, he began
to sell copies of his poems from door to door and thought of
himself as a wandering minstrel. He worked at the Y.M.C.A.,
lectured to young people on art and took parties of them to
the Metropolitan Museum. He was usually able to earn only
ten dollars a week, but for several years he kept up these interests, lecturing at four settlement houses as well.

But from his mother the would-be poet inherited great rest-
lessness. He finally left New York to go on a walking tour
through the South. In March 1906 he sailed to Jacksonville,
Florida, with a friend. They planned to walk back north.
Later Vachel walked alone through Florida, Georgia, North
Carolina, Tennessee and Kentucky, covering six hundred
miles. In his *A Handy Guide for Beggars* he recorded how he
preached his "Gospel of Beauty" at cabins and farmhouses as
he went along; and he would read his poems to anyone who
cared to listen. This journey, he felt, put him in touch with
his native land. His burning wish was to make all America
sensitive to the beauty of poetry.

Meantime the elder Lindsays resolved to make an effort to
divert their son from his impractical pursuits and that same
year they took him and his sister Joy to Europe. However
straitened they might be, there always seemed to be money
put by for travel. They visited England, Holland, Belgium,
Germany and France. Though Vachel appeared to enjoy certain aspects of the trip, he remained obdurate and went on

another poetic tour upon his return, covering New York, New Jersey and Pennsylvania in much the same way as he had previously covered the South. At long last he came back to Springfield which he had always loved. But his ideas made him unpopular there. He had conceived a definite philosophy of life founded on democracy, beauty and holiness. He saw hopes of this in the smaller American towns. So he commenced to work with the Anti-Saloon League in central Illinois and in talks to the Y.M.C.A. in Springfield. He campaigned busily against industrialism and greed; he printed his *Village Magazine*. For this paper he wrote articles and poems and drew pictures to explain them. But he was known among his townsfolk as an eccentric.

In May 1912, when he was thirty-three, Vachel went on a preaching trip through the West. He carried a pamphlet, *Rhymes to Be Traded for Bread*, and a leaflet of his *Gospel of Beauty*, also a little book of famous characters and beautiful places. He was poor and had to work hard for meals and lodging, often making but a few cents a day. In some way he felt himself a part of these western farms. On one farm he saw a young colt cruelly abused until it died; he remembered the scene and wrote "The Broncho That Would Not Be Broken."

Now the tide began to turn. In the fall of that year, 1912, the *American Magazine* actually published "The Proud Farmer," a portrait of Vachel's grandfather, and in January 1913 Harriet Monroe's new magazine, *Poetry*, brought out his remarkable new poem, the cry of an evangelist called "General William Booth Enters into Heaven." It made a great impression on the literary world of both New York and London. The author went on to Chicago and met his editor, Harriet Monroe, and many of his peers among the poets.

Now he entered on the most successful part of his career—the recitals of his poems to thousands of people. Vachel Lindsay had a deep and melodious voice and took to chanting his work at colleges, women's clubs and other groups. All at once he made his mark and became a celebrity, a striking figure with blue-gray eyes, light hair and a bulging forehead. When he recited his poetry, he raised his face, half closed his eyes and used theatrical gestures. The poems that lent themselves most successfully to this style of delivery were "The Congo," "General William Booth Enters into Heaven" and the "Kallyope Yell." But this form of recital told heavily on his heart.

Three books of his poems followed each other swiftly, *The Congo and Other Poems* in 1913, *The Chinese Nightingale* in 1917 and *The Golden Whales of California* in 1920. In 1923 his *Collected Poems* appeared. But the great disappointment in poor Vachel Lindsay's career was that he could not give his huge audiences the ideals for which he cared so deeply. He could not preach his Gospel of Beauty to them; they would not have listened. They wanted their "Jazz Poet," as they called him, to entertain them. As time went on this work grew harder and harder, less of a novelty—and the audiences shrank.

Vachel lost his father in 1920, and he and his mother went on a tour to England where he was most warmly received and recognized by John Masefield, Robert Bridges, Robert Graves, Robert Nichols, William Butler Yeats, John Drinkwater and a host of others. Graves, in speaking of his performance at Oxford, said afterward: "Lindsay was a most staggering success." He was thought of everywhere and mentioned as the great American poet. But the time came to sail home and return to Springfield where the town gave a banquet in his honor. His mother died of pneumonia two short years later and her death was a tremendous blow. In settling the family estate he lost his home, the house he cared for so much.

For a short time Vachel had a resident poet's position at Gulf Park College in Gulfport, Mississippi, but he did not care for the cold atmosphere of this college and moved to Spokane, Washington, finding congenial friends there and, most of all, his wife, Elizabeth Conner, a writer. They were married in 1925 and for a while were happy, but two children had come and they had financial problems. The homesick husband and father thought they would do better in Springfield where he was known, so they moved East. But when they came home, though enabled to live in his own house, Vachel's resources were gone. He had debts, knew that he had become an ill man, had lost his vogue as a poet and was greatly discouraged. He did not know which way to turn. The night of December 5th, 1931 he suddenly died. His town, which had not honored him greatly in life, honored him in death and buried him close to the tomb of his hero, Lincoln. He was a compassionate idealist and we think of him with sympathy, for his life should not have ended as it did.

His poems for children are among his most delightful ventures. The young love the sweep and roar of *The Congo*. But they also love the fanciful poems, "The Moon's the North Wind's Cooky," "The Little Turtle," "Dirge for a Righteous Kitten," "The Mysterious Cat," "The Grasshopper," "The Potatoes Dance," "Crickets on a Strike." One of these is quoted here:

THE MOON'S THE NORTH WIND'S COOKY
(WHAT THE LITTLE GIRL SAID)

The Moon's the North Wind's cooky.
He bites it, day by day,

Until there's but a rim of scraps
That crumble all away.

The South Wind is a baker,
And kneads clouds in his den,
And bakes a crisp new moon *that . . . greedy*
North . . . Wind . . . eats . . . again!

ELEANOR FARJEON

[1881–   ]

ELEANOR FARJEON, an English writer for children, passionately loved growing things in the English countryside. Yet she was born in the Strand in London, the third child and only daughter of B. L. Farjeon, the novelist, and Margaret Jefferson, the eldest daughter of Joseph Jefferson, the famous American actor who, among his other achievements, numbered an immortal performance of Rip Van Winkle. Two brothers, Harry and Charlie, were older than "Nellie," as she was called, and two, Joseph Jefferson and Herbert, were younger. Charlie died as a baby and the three boys and one girl grew up together. Considering the stiff Victorian age they lived in, these children had an unusual bringing up with a gay, gentle mother and a whimsical and very impulsive father. The routine of a regular education for his children did not appeal to him, and Nellie never went to school but absorbed learning from a succession of nursery governesses who were told not to bother her because she had headaches. In *A Nursery in the Nineties* which is part of her entrancing book, *Portrait of a Family*, Nellie gives a picture of a bewildered, just-engaged governess, who tells her mother at the end of the day that she had been ordered to take the children to the zoo instead of giving them lessons. The house had to be kept quiet for Mr. Farjeon's work. "Well," responded her mother, "You can but try it." She did try and succeeded in winning the children's interest and affection.

The parents' world was the Bohemian one of literature and drama. Consequently the children met interesting and notable people and were taken to the theater and opera from the time Nellie was four. At seven years old she was composing on the typewriter, and as soon as she could read she had her father's huge library to browse in. All four children began early to produce magazine poems, plays and stories. The director of their lives was Harry, the oldest brother. "I did not need a nurse," said the children's mother when questioned. "I had Harry." He disciplined his clan by a certain code of rigid justice, but there were many treats as well. No one of them would have thought of neglecting to wash his hands for meals or to go to bed promptly after Harry had given the signal for these duties. The generous father often turned holiday parties into real fairy tales. Perhaps he was a bit of a grown-up child himself. The four called themselves "Harry, Nellie, Joe and Bertie" and as such stood against the world.

Harry, at an early age, showed that he had brilliant and unusual musical gifts. When he entered the Royal Academy of Music he continued to take scholarships and prizes. But it was his sister, Nellie, who supplied him with books for the various operas that he composed. When she was sixteen, the Academy of Music gave a performance in a public hall, an opera done by one of its students. The title was "Floretta," a love of Henry of Navarre, and Nellie had turned the story into verse which her brother had set to music. "I made my first public bow," she says, in *Junior Book of Authors* "at sixteen in pigtails . . but except for a blank verse poem on Chaos, none of my early work was good."

It is no wonder that they were musical and literary. The children's mother sang them all the American songs that she had grown up with, and by the time Nellie was ten, her father presented each child with a book every Sunday after dinner. Nellie's first one was Tennyson's *In Memoriam* and she always remembered that her father talked with her about the author and read his poetry aloud. Shakespeare was the children's favorite, however.

Whenever Nellie Farjeon wrote a poem or story, she ran to push the manuscript under her father's study door. Even when he was busily writing, he would notice the little missive —and later come up to the nursery to talk with her about it, point out flaws or encourage her. She said, "I always had stomach-ache till I heard whether he liked it or not." Once when she was ill in bed, she wrote a twenty-thousand-word story to be submitted for a prize. Sending it downstairs to her father, she waited in fear and trembling for the verdict. After a while he came upstairs and said to her, no doubt smiling: "Well, Nell, I have hopes of you, I have hopes of you." She was content and no longer worried about the prize. Her father really felt that she might be a writer and that was what she wanted to be.

When she lost her father in 1903, Nellie was twenty-two. Their grandfather, Joseph Jefferson, who had never seen the children, sent for them all to come to America the following year, to his home at Buzzards Bay, Massachusetts. Nellie thought this visit a revelation of a new world which was peopled by delightful cousins, uncles and aunts. The Farjeons might have decided to make America their home, but Harry had just received his appointment as a professor of harmony and composition at the Royal Academy. This took the family back to England and two years later their grandfather died.

Nellie continued with her writing at home but slowly, no doubt plumbing, as someone once said, "the virgin forest of her mind." She did not produce much of note until the First World War when her first successes were with two series of *Nursery Rhymes of London Town.* Set to simple tunes of her own making, they had the honor, later on, of being sung in most of London's junior schools. When air raids threatened London, Nellie took a laborer's cottage in Sussex to avoid the effects on her mother. Here, as she later related, she worked in the garden, cooked, gathered all her own firewood, raced on the downs and wrote the charming *Martin Pippin in the Apple Orchard.* When it was published she felt she had found herself. It was at this time, too, that she became an intimate friend of Edward Thomas, the young English poet, and his family before his tragic death in the war.

After the war ended and the laborer claimed his cottage, Nellie lived near her delicate mother in London. Later she discovered to her delight a fascinating cottage in Hampstead with a Queen Anne garden. So for twelve years until her mother's death in 1933 she divided her time between this loved home and her mother's house in London. Those years were full as she constantly wrote poems, music, children's stories and games, a novel, plays and what she called "fantastic fiction."

Then came World War II and she returned to London in 1940 to be near her brothers during the Battle of Britain. Herbert was the brother who collaborated with her in her book, *Kings and Queens,* from whose amusing pages children will readily and easily recall the successive reigns in English history. But Herbert died in 1945 just after the highly successful performance of their musical play, "The Glass Slipper." When

Harry died three years later, after peace was declared, Nellie Farjeon made Hampstead her home. In 1951 she joined the Catholic Church.

In appearance she is said to be "dark-haired and rosy" with a genuine and deep zest for everything in life. Her poems for children are skilfully written, for she is an excellent craftsman and many of her rhythms are as "lively as a dance." Of her fairy poems, *City-Under-the-Water* is perhaps the prettiest, and she knows how to amuse children with her own brand of unique nonsense. Her principal works form a lengthy list:

Martin Pippin in the Apple Orchard, 1922; *Soul of Kol Nikon*, 1923; *Mighty Men*, 1925; *Italian Peep Show and Other Tales*, 1926; *Joan's Door*, 1927; *Come Christmas*, 1928; *Collection of Poems*, 1929; *Faithful Jenny Dove and Other Tales*, 1929; *The King's Daughter Cries for the Moon*, 1929; *Westwards*, 1930; *Young Gerard*, 1930; *Ladybrook*, 1931; *Fair of St. James*, 1932; *Katy Kruse at the Seaside*, 1932; *Ameliaranne and the Magic Ring*, 1933; *Ameliaranne's Washing Day*, 1934; *Jim at the Corner and Other Stories*, 1934; *A Nursery in the Nineties* (in *Portrait of A Family*), 1935; *Jim and the Pirates*, 1936; *Two Bouquets* (with Herbert Farjeon), 1936; *Wonders of Horodotus*, 1937; *Martin Pippin in the Daisy Field*, 1938; *One Foot in Fairyland*, 1938; *Granny Gray* (musical play) 1939; *A Sussex Alphabet*, 1939; *Miss Granby's Secret March*, 1941; and many others. Her poems on Christmas should be mentioned as especially touching and significant.

One of the most engaging of her poems is quoted here:

THE NIGHT WILL NEVER STAY

The night will never stay,
The night will still go by,

Though with a million stars
You pin it to the sky,
Though you bind it to the blowing wind
And buckle it with the moon,
The night will slip away
Like sorrow or a tune.

ALAN ALEXANDER MILNE

[1882–1956]

A. A. MILNE, who wrote the Christopher Robin books and *Winnie-the-Pooh*, must have been a bright and alert little boy, to judge by his autobiography. He was born in London, England, the son of John Vine Milne, who not only ran a private school for boys called Henley House but was an excellent teacher and playfellow of his three boys. Though they had a good mother, the father seems to have been the one who managed their lives and laid down the rules they followed. Alan and his brother Kenneth, sixteen months older, were inseparable, and his account of their childhood with all its pranks and adventures is enthralling. Both small boys had long fair hair and wore lace collars through their early years, for the time was the Lord Fauntleroy period.

Both Alan and his brother won scholarships to Westminster School where, with a reputation as a mathematical genius, Alan after one year stopped working and took his studies very easily. While at Westminster, Alan and another boy were examining an undergraduate magazine from Cambridge called the *Granta*. "You ought to edit this," said the other boy. "I will," replied young Milne. Strangely enough, he went to Cambridge when everyone expected him to go to Oxford, and he did edit the *Granta*. In 1903, at twenty-one, he got his degree and then notified his astonished parents that he was not going into teaching or the Indian civil service but planned to become a journalist in London. He had enough money left from his Cambridge allowance to support himself for a year.

At the end of the year he had spent all his money and had earned, by writing, a beggarly twenty pounds. So he moved from his expensive rooms into cheap and dirty ones in the house of a policeman in Chelsea—and went on writing. The second year of the writing experiment he made one hundred and twenty pounds and lived on it. In the third year he was making two hundred pounds, for several papers had become interested in his contributions and, as he said, "were getting used to me." In February 1906 at twenty-four he had a surprise. He was offered the assistant editorship of *Punch*, accepted and stayed with it until the end of 1914—eight years.

Then World War I broke out and Milne joined the Royal Warwickshire Regiment. A year before he had married Dorothy (called Daphne) de Sélincourt, who was also a writer. While he was in training camp he wrote a fairy play in which both he and his wife acted together with other soldiers and their wives. By this time Milne had already published three volumes of his essays from *Punch* and people were beginning to know him as a humorist. When he was sent to the Western Front he actually found time to write a play that bore the extraordinary name of "Wurzel-Flummery."

Soon after this he was wounded and invalided and on his return was made signaling instructor at a camp in England. During this time he wrote three more plays and by the time he was demobilized he was well enough known as a writer to resign from *Punch* and give all his time to writing books. His small boy, Christopher Robin (who was always by his own request called Billy Moon or Billy), became the hero of a whole series of verses, stories and plays, including the books dealing with Winnie-the-Pooh. Winnie-the-Pooh was a small teddy bear who came to Christopher Robin when he was a year old. They were exactly the same size, became devoted companions and used to roll and tumble together on the nursery floor. In writing the book about the little bear, Christopher Robin's father used the names of all the nursery animals his son was so fond of—Piglet, Eeyore, the gray donkey, Kanga Roo and others. Ernest Shepherd, the artist, who was to make the pictures for the book, came to call respectfully on all the animals. Milne's whimsical verses became so popular that they threatened to overthrow his more serious work as a playwright. Thousands of people knew his verses who never heard of his comedies. *Changing Guard at Buckingham Palace* might be better known than *Mr. Pim Passes By*, *The Dover Road* and *The Truth About Blayds*, plays which are, however, very well liked. Mr. Milne also wrote *The Red House Mystery*, a highly successful mystery play.

He was tall, tanned and athletic looking, with alert blue eyes, and reminded one of Barrie minus Barrie's genius. He was genuinely witty and an adept at satire. He lived until 1956 and must have enjoyed everything connected with his Christopher Robin. Mr. Milne always said, oddly enough, that the verses were not actually written to Christopher Robin but to some imaginary child or to all children, including himself. He did not intend to direct them to his son.

His plays are too many to be listed here. His novels are: *Mr. Pim*, 1921; *The Red House Mystery*, 1921; *Two People*, 1931; *Four Days Wonder*, 1933. His juvenile books are: *When We Were Very Young*, 1924; *Winnie-the-Pooh*, 1926; *Now We Are Six*, 1927; *The House at Pooh Corner*, 1928; *The*

Christopher Robin Reader, 1929; *The Christopher Robin Birthday Book,* 1931; *The Christopher Robin Verses,* 1932; and other books including his fascinating *Autobiography,* 1939, and *Behind the Lines* (verse), 1940.

Merely quoting a stanza of the famous *Changing Guard at Buckingham Palace* will bring to countless thousands of readers, young and old, the rhymes of the king who only wanted a bit of butter for the royal slice of bread, the doctor who gave Christopher what goes with a cold in the nose and many other lilting poems which have become the heritage of childhood everywhere.

> They're changing guard at Buckingham Palace—
> Christopher Robin went down with Alice.
> "Do you think the King knows all about me?"
> "Sure to, dear, but it's time for tea,"
> > Says Alice.

RACHEL LYMAN FIELD

[1894–1942]

$\mathcal{R}$ACHEL LYMAN FIELD, one of the most cherished of children's writers in her generation, was born in New York City, the fourth daughter of Matthew Field and Lucy Atwater, and a great-niece of the famous Cyrus West Field who laid the first Atlantic submarine cable. Of several children, only she and an older sister survived. Her mother, early widowed, took her two young children to Stockbridge, Massachusetts, where Rachel's childhood up to the age of ten was spent in a simple, friendly New England country village atmosphere. She went to a small school kept by two old ladies and later said that she was lazy and did not care for reading, spelling or arithmetic. But from the first she showed a true love of poetry and a desire to act in plays. Though Rachel did not read fluently until she was more than ten, she was only nine when she played Shylock in the *Merchant of Venice* at the school's Christmas play and the leading rôle in *Rebecca of Sunnybrook Farm* in the June performance. Though she could not read the parts, they were read to her and she decided in her own mind that she would be a great actress.

She and her sister Elizabeth, as little children, were taken as a treat on Sunday evenings to hear the orphans in the orphan asylum in town sing hymns and patriotic songs. "Yankee Doodle" was a tremendous favorite. One day Rachel, seated on a chair, was holding a heavy book of fine engravings on her small lap. Of course the volume slipped, fell to the floor and several pages were badly crumpled. Coming in at this moment and viewing the damage, her mother said: "Oh, Rachel, you do try me so with this carelessness. I get *so* discouraged."

Rachel looked up, not in the least troubled. "You must never be discouraged," she answered brightly. "Take it to the Lord in prayer and call it"—she paused an instant—"*macaroni!*"

The year she was ten, Mrs. Field thought Rachel needed the drill of a good public school. So the Fields moved to Springfield, Massachusetts. But Rachel never caught up with the group of her age in school work, though she wrote other pupils' compositions for them as well as composing her own. She began to experiment in writing herself and occasionally had her efforts printed in the school paper or by the St. Nicholas League. This last, she said, gave her the best of training and discipline. Her graduation from high school seemed very doubtful, but Rachel won an essay prize for which three schools competed and was allowed to graduate. It was then that she decided she wanted to write.

By an arrangement not possible in this day and time she was admitted to Radcliffe College as a special student. During her last two years there she was in Professor George P. Baker's "English 47," the playwriting course where the students wrote their own plays. Rachel wrote a short play, "Three Pills in a Bottle," and received much encouragement about it. Later it was published in a group, became highly popular and was played throughout the country.

When college was behind her, Rachel Field, like so many

others, went on to New York to seek her fortune. At first she did jobs for the editorial department of Lasky's Famous Players, writing synopses of plays and books for the motion pictures. But in her leisure moments she wrote short plays, verse and a novel. Though the novel was never accepted, editors told its young author that the best part of the book was the descriptions of childhood and advised her to do more in that vein. It is interesting to note that an editor on the *New York Evening Post*, for whose pages she reviewed books, said: "I do like to see Miss Field come in. She is like a big, sunny, country child, bringing fresh flowers."

Her first mild success was a book of verses and silhouettes called *The Pointed People* which was accepted by the Yale University Press. It happened to come out when A. A. Milne's *When We Were Very Young* was sweeping the country, yet it was kept in print. Then Scribner's brought out Rachel's first book of one-act plays and Macmillan accepted *Eliza and the Elves*, graced with Elizabeth MacKinstry's charming illustrations. Other small books followed—*An Alphabet for Boys and Girls* and *Polly Patchwork* which Rachel illustrated herself with simple pictures. *Little Dog Toby* was suggested, the author said, by a dog she saw in a Punch-and-Judy show in London in 1926. Two years later Rachel happened to discover a little wooden doll in an antique shop. Straightway she and her friend, the well-known illustrator, Dorothy Lathrop, planned this doll's story. Rachel decided to use in it her knowledge of early American life and the descriptions of whaling she had picked up in Maine, where she spent her summers. Dorothy made the pictures, the book being sent on to her, chapter by chapter. *Hitty* published by Louise Seaman of Macmillan's proved to be a unique doll book and was awarded the Newbery Medal for the most distinguished juvenile for 1929. This reward was a turning point in Rachel's career.

One of the most real sources of her imaginative writing was the island in Maine, a small and rare place where she owned a cottage, Sutton Island, opposite Seal Harbor and upon whose untouched shore no car was allowed to come. The cottagers had speed boats to reach the mainland for their shopping. The island abounded in crimson toadstools, charming minute flowers and mosses which made a suitable diminutive setting for elves and fairies. It was no wonder that all these tiny mysteries went into her books or that *Hitty* and *Calico Bush* possessed much of the loved and familiar setting of that coast which was roots and background to her. *Hitty* was pronounced to be the only true juvenile classic written in America in a generation, and its publicity and sale were enormous.

It was a loss to children's literature when Rachel Field turned to writing adult fiction and deserted the children's field, though her two novels, *Time Out of Mind* and *All This and Heaven Too* were popular successes and found their way into moving pictures. The second book was based on the life of a great-aunt by marriage, Henriettes Deluzy-Desportes, who married Rachel's great-uncle, the Reverend Henry Field. This distant relative was the central figure of a famous murder story in 1847.

Besides writing, Rachel was interested in cooking, and in designing and making gifts for her friends. Her New York apartment, furnished in her own style, was like no one else's. There were period pictures, mottoes on the walls, gay old quilts. A tall schoolmaster's desk worthy of Ichabod Crane stood in a corner, there was a case of ancient dolls of every variety, plus music boxes, especially one prized music box that resembled a workbasket. It had once belonged to Mary Webb, the English author of *Precious Bane*.

In 1935 Rachel Field married Arthur Pedersen, a Swede and a literary agent. Years later, because of opportunities opening up in California, they moved there and had one daughter, Hannah. Rachel wrote some charming verses for this loved child and no doubt, as Hannah grew, they would have been followed by more delightful story books. "Life," it was said of Rachel, "flowed in her like spring sap and she had a faculty of communicating that superb vitality to all who touched her." No human being was ever gifted with keener powers of enjoyment. But she could also be overwhelmingly sad at times.

She lived modestly in a house in Beverly Hills, California, and her immense success did not alter her quiet way of life among the Hollywood stars. She had a wealth of curly auburn hair, blue eyes, a wide, generous mouth and a merry, contagious laugh. There was a robustness about her personality and her work. She was a good and staunch friend, always insisting on taking the man's part and paying herself for what was supposed to be a mutual entertainment. "To see her often," said an acquaintance, "was to welcome Christmas." Her sunny life was cut short in 1942 by an operation from which she never recovered. She was buried in the old family plot at Stockbridge—and that same year *The Horn Book* devoted an entire issue to her life and writings. Her principal books are: *Hitty—Her First Hundred Years, The Pointed People, Taxis and Toadstools, A Little Book of Days, Eliza and the Elves, Little Dog Toby, The Magic Pawnshop, Six Plays, Calico Bush, Hepatica Hawkes, Branches Green, Fear Is the Thorn, God's Pocket, Points East, Time Out of Mind, All This and Heaven Too, Now Tomorrow.*

Here are four lines from one of her children's poems.

WILD CRANBERRY

Were these the fairy apples Snow-White knew,
Scarlet-sided and white?
And shall these lips of mine taste magic too,
And spells, at the first sharp bite?

STEPHEN VINCENT BENÉT

[1898–1943]

ROSEMARY CARR BENÉT

[1898–1962]

STEPHEN VINCENT BENÉT and his wife, Rosemary Carr, were often called by their friends "the last of the romantics." There never were two people who worked more harmoniously and happily than these two over *A Book of Americans*. Both possessed much originality and their mutual exchange of ideas was felicitous. Perhaps they never thought of the rôle of children's poets until they began to create the varied and clever rhymes for their new scheme of a book.

Their backgrounds were quite different. Stephen Vincent Benét was born on July 22, 1898, in Bethlehem, Pennsylvania, the second son and youngest child of Captain James Walker Benét, United States Army, and Frances Neill Rose. Rosemary Carr was born in Chicago on January 14, 1898, the only child of Thomas Carr and his wife, Rachel Hickey. They met in Paris during the fall and winter of 1920. Rosemary was doing fashion and feature work on the Paris edition of the *New York Herald Tribune*, and Stephen, having received a traveling fellowship from Yale, was studying at the Sorbonne. They fell in love at first sight. After their engagement they returned to the land of their birth and were married in December 1921. At the time the entertaining *Book of Americans* was planned they were the parents of three promising children, Stephanie, Thomas Carr and Rachel Felicity, so pleasantly mentioned in the book's dedication. By this time, too, Stephen had made a lasting reputation with his famous saga of *John Brown's Body*.

Stephen Benét was deeply and powerfully interested in his America, her legends, her songs, her explorers, her public men. As a small, delicate boy of seven he had first crossed the continent with his mother, brother and sister. The sweep of the country, the mighty rivers, the prairies, Great Salt Lake, the trail of the Covered Wagons, the Rocky Mountains in sight at last, made a permanent impression upon a young, sensitive and growing mind, as the train rolled on to California where his family was joining the husband and father at Benicia. Benicia had been named for the wife of the Spanish general, Vallejo, and was once the capital of the state of California. Stephen's mother, who greatly enjoyed travel and had a great enthusiasm for her country, gave her three children a never-to-be-forgotten experience on this long journey. There was a little platform at the end of the train where they sat, and Stephen listened with interest to his mother's stories as they moved along. On the last morning, when the California border was crossed, all the travelers feasted on freshly caught mountain trout and newly picked raspberries!

Stephen spent six years in Benicia, and when the next change in the Benéts' home territory came in 1911, it was to Augusta, Georgia, in the far South. So Stephen very early in life became familiar with another piece of his great American map and realized, with dramatic force, the stories of North and South that were to appear in his *John Brown's Body*, published in 1928.

He and Rosemary had been married twelve years when on a day in May 1933 Stephen happened to go to the New York Public Library and saw there what he termed "a superb collection" of children's books, including Eleanor Farjeon's pictorial *Kings and Queens*. Money was scarce at that time. Stephen and John Farrar, his close friend and publisher, lunched together and discussed the idea of a new book of juvenile verse which Stephen thought of calling *Presidents and People*. He talked it over with his wife and they decided to make the book a mutual affair. He had been working that winter on a novel, *James Shore's Daughter*. He was somewhat held up on that work and wanted to shift to something lighter. Verse would be a relief.

Both he and Rosemary realized that this book must have the best in the way of illustrations. They thought of their friend, Charlie Child, the illustrator, just back from Paris and living in Bucks County, Pennyslvania. Child thought their plan a good one and made some sketches which promised well. Then Stephen and Rosemary divided up their characters of men and women, he to write the rhymes about the males, she those about the women. Every day for the next two weeks Stephen did one of the verses and sometimes two. Child found him most flexible and easy to work with both as author and collaborator —and said so.

That summer when the Benéts were renting the Hazard estate at Peace Dale, Rhode Island, Charlie Child drove up to see them. More sketches were gone over and discussed. Occasionally he would make a drawing first and Stephen would then write the verse to suit it. What they aimed for was "plenty of snap and bite" in both text and illustrations. Stephen worked very hard on some of the verse. The poems on Lincoln and Lee were rewritten again and again. Others flowed easily to him. Both he and Rosemary especially admired Thomas Jefferson, having visited often in both Richmond and Charlottesville:

> They call you rascal?
> They called me worse.
> You'd do grand things, sir,
> But lack the purse?
>
> I got no riches,
> I died a debtor.
> I died free-hearted
> And that was better.
>
> For life was freakish
> But life was fervent.
> And I was always
> Life's willing servant.
>
> Life, life's too weighty?
> Too long a haul, sir?
> I lived past eighty,
> I liked it all, sir.

"John James Audubon" was another charming and amusing poem. Rosemary was the author of "Jesse James" and the poem "Nancy Hanks" that has so stirred boys, girls and adults in both schools and radio performances. Its words are exactly the words a long dead mother would have spoken in asking about her lost son:

"You wouldn't know
About my son?
Did he grow tall?
Did he have fun?
Did he learn to read?
Did he get to town?
Do you know his name?
Did he get on?"

"Negro Spirituals" was more than a verse. It was a touching poem. Its rhythm rolled like a chant. The book ended with
P. T. Barnum in his glory, the Wright Brothers and Robert
Peary. It was a lively and informative young volume, an
astonishing collection of the simple, the serious and the comic,
and its authors chose as a title for it: A Book of Americans.
Through July and August of that summer they worked dili-
gently, preparing the volume for fall publication. By mid-
September both verse and pictures were ready and in October
the limited edition was signed. Stephen had written the characteristic dedication: "To Stephanie, Tom and Rachel, our
other works in collaboration."

On Armistice Day, 1933, the trade edition of *A Book of
Americans*, published by Farrar and Rinehart, appeared and
had good reviews. Both the enchanting pictures and the entertaining verses made a hit and the book sold surprisingly well.
Passages from it were quoted in anthologies, reprinted in
columns such as F.P.A.'s "The Conning Tower," put into
Braille, and several of the verses were set to music. The Benéts
could never have imagined the immense popularity their book
of children's verse would have in the public schools. Recitations, pantomimes and plays were drawn from it. No doubt
many a student who was inclined to take his work easily,
learned American history from its pages. It is a matter for

regret that the authors never seemed to have time or inclination to do more poems for children.

Here is one of the most amusing verses, that on Captain Kidd.

CAPTAIN KIDD

The person in the gaudy clothes
Is worthy Captain Kidd
They say he never buried gold,
I think perhaps he did.

They say it's all a story that
His favorite little song
Was "Make these lubbers walk the plank"!
I think perhaps they're wrong.

They say he never pirated
Beneath the Skull-and-Bones.
But merely traveled for his health
And spoke in soothing tones.
In fact, you'll read in nearly all
The newer history books
That he was mild as cottage cheese
But I don't like his looks.

THOMAS AUGUSTINE DALY

[1871–1948]

A NEWSPAPERMAN known for his popular verse in the Italian vernacular, Thomas Augustine Daly was born in Philadelphia, the son of John Anthony Daly and Anne Victoria. He was educated at Villanova College and Fordham University. In later years Fordham gave him a Litt.D. and Notre Dame University an LL.D. His first job was as a clerk on the Philadelphia *Record*, then as a reporter, then as a special writer from 1889 to 1898. Later he became general manager of the *Catholic Standard and Times* from 1898 to 1915 and greatly revived that moribund sheet. He was a columnist for the Philadelphia *Evening Ledger* from 1915 to 1918 and later an editorial writer for the *Evening Bulletin*. In 1905 he developed his ability as a lecturer and after-dinner speaker and traveled over his own country and Canada as well as parts of England.

Meantime he had become a pioneer in the writing of Italian dialect verse and gave animated recitals of his work. His first book, *Canzoni*, was published in 1906 and sold fifty thousand copies. It was followed by *Carmina*, *Madrigali* and *McAroni Ballads* as well as two books of prose. "Tom" Daly, as Christopher Morley and Joyce Kilmer called him, was, like many humorists, rather solemn looking with deep-set eyes behind spectacles and of medium height. He was most happily married and had eight children, five sons and three daughters. He writes of them all in his delightful "Herself and the Houseful," also in an exquisite poem called "The Thrush" about a little crippled daughter. That poem took the second "Lyric Year" prize in a contest and the money its author received went toward a new house for the whole family.

Daly's boys must have gloried in the fact that their father during his college days was second-string pitcher and outfielder at Villanova and short stop at Fordham University, as well as quarterback of the football team until incapacitated by an injury. And what fun their clever father must have had reading Italian ditties with his enormous family as an audience!

Daly was a founder of the Poor Richard Club of Philadelphia and a charter member of the American Press Humorists and president from 1906 to 1907, also for many years a member of the Authors Club and the Players. F.P.A. always called him "Daly, the Troubadour," and Christopher Morley said of him: "He has found good in simple hearts and flowers growing round the heavy wheelbarrows of journalism." Daly himself said of his work: "I have had more pleasure in the writing of many of these simple songs than the reading of them could possibly give to the public."

Louis Untermeyer noted that Daly was less popular than James Whitcomb Riley or Paul Lawrence Dunbar. "Daly," he said, "is more skilful and versatile than either; his range and quality are comparable to Eugene Field's." Here is one of his gems:

CARLOTTA'S DECISION

I would lika mooch to know
Why Carlotta treat me so.

Evra time I ask eef she
Ees 'gon marry weetha me,
First she smile, den she frown,
Den she look me up an' down,
Den she shak' her head an' say:
"I gon' tal you Chrees'mas Day."

Once w'en we are out for walk
An' I am begin to talk,
She say: "Don'ta speak no more.
O! com' see dees jew'ler store.
My! jus' look dat di'mon' reeng!
Eet ees justa sweetes' theeng!
Only seexa-feefty, see?"
Dat's de way she teases me,
Findin' theengs for talk 'bout
Jus' for mak' me shut my mout!
Bimeby w'en she turn for go
I say "Com,' I musta know,"—
"O!" she stamp her foot and say:
"I gon' tal you Chrees'mas Day."

I would lika mooch to know
Why Carlotta treat me so.
W'ata for she always say,
"I gon' tal you Chrees'mas Day?"

ALFRED NOYES

[1880–1958]

THE ENGLISH poet, Alfred Noyes, was born in Wolverhampton, Staffordshire, England, on September 16, 1880, the son of Alfred and Amelia Adams Noyes. Like Swinburne, his early days were passed by the sea and in the hills of Wales. A true poet is certainly born, not made. Poetry was literally born and fostered in this boy by his discovery, on a steep mountainside, of a sunlit space within a wood only about twelve feet in diameter. In his autobiography, *Two Worlds*, the author says: "Above it there were great boulders of rock encrusted with golden lichen, and over the tops of the young fir trees that guarded its other three sides it commanded a wide prospect, a valley with a river winding down to a long and lonely coast line and west of this coast line 'the immeasurable tremor of all the sea.' "

In this quiet mountain nook where he was undisturbed the springs of poetry began to rise for him. He must have been about twelve at the time and to this cherished spot he carried his first copy of Spenser's *The Faerie Queene* and a few other books of poetry. He was reading, reading continually. He kept a diary in which he jotted down the names of the books, and in it were Ballentyne's *Coral Island* and the works of Henry,

138

Cooper, Mark Twain, Stevenson and almost the whole of Dickens. He says: "There was also a series of twopenny colored penny dreadfuls in which Deadwood Dick had blood-curdling adventures among cowboys and Indians." These stories were the germ of Noyes' rousing poem, "The High-wayman."

The fagging and continual flogging of English schoolboy life were not for young Alfred. He went as a day boy to a small private school near his home, Jasper House School, run by a Mr. Pope, a Cambridge man who took only twelve boarders and twenty-five day boys. Alfred, unlike many young poets, played football and cricket and entered swimming contests, for swimming was a sport he loved. In the holidays he had a small sailing boat of his own and went sea fishing but never without a book in his pocket.

An amusing tale of his boyhood is that of the quaint judgment that an austerely kind uncle, a clergyman, meted out to him and his cousin Herbert. The two boys had been playing Red Indians and Herbert hit Alfred a violent whack with a tomahawk which gave him a bleeding head. Later, at Sunday dinner, which the children shared with their elders, Alfred appeared in bandages and sentence was passed upon Herbert by his father. He was to have no pudding at the midday meal for a whole week. So Herbert's plate was empty when dessert was served. Suddenly his uncle said to Alfred (who had just received a generous help of pudding on account of the accident), "Now would you like to give an example of self-sacrifice?" Not knowing what it was, Alfred said yes, and his uncle transferred his plate of pudding to his cousin—while he received no second helping. This sacrifice went on for a week, and the victim realized that if he had tomahawked his cousin Herbert, he would have had the pudding.

Alfred's father was a kind, gentle and deeply religious man. Like his two brothers, he had longed ardently to go into the church—but was disappointed in that ambition and later was kept from professional life by an invalid wife who could not share any activity. His devotion to her was supreme and it was he who brought up his two boys and encouraged Alfred in his early efforts at poetry.

From Jasper House he went on to Exeter College, Oxford, where all went well with him, except that in his rowing feats he never became a "blue." He had an excellent tutor, Marett by name, who took a great interest in him, telling him, no doubt with a twinkle in his eye, that his best college work would probably be done in vacations. However, young Noyes, in company with other undergraduates, formed an Essay Club where the members wrote weekly papers on English poets of their choice. No one penned a paper on an author he cared nothing about. This was excellent training and Alfred did an immense amount of reading. But in the fourth and last year of college, when he was about to graduate and had just completed his first book of poems, an important letter came to him from London. The letter was from the publisher to whom he had sent his manuscript, inviting the young author to come to see him in London and discuss the book, which he evidently liked. The offer was tempting; the final examinations were not. Noyes cut the examinations, thus losing his degree—though his college honored him later on. Instead of a degree he produced in 1902 a book of poems, *The Loom of Years*. He says: "Somewhat to my surprise I incurred no blame from the University authorities." Few young writers have been more fortunate.

"The Highwayman," that romantic poem of Alfred Noyes that every boy (and girl, too) finds exciting and moving with its swinging ballad meter was written in two days in a small cottage on the edge of Bagshot Heath, where its twenty-four-year-old creator had taken rooms soon after he left Oxford. He says in *Two Worlds for Memory* "Bagshot Heath in those days was a wild bit of country, all heather and pine woods." "The Highwayman" suggested itself to its author "one blustery night when the sound of the wind in the pines gave him the first line." This poem has been reprinted in many anthologies and in several hundred schoolbooks in both England and America. It has been broadcast repeatedly and was made eventually into a Hollywood cinema.

Meanwhile a letter of recommendation from George Meredith, novelist and poet who approved of young Noyes' poems, pushed that young man ahead when he went up to London. Apparently he had no difficulty in getting his work before the public and even making his living. But then, living was cheap in those days. Noyes' "The Phantom Fleet" occupied pages in *Blackwood's* magazine, and the long poem "Drake" (which letters from Robert Louis Stevenson had encouraged him to undertake) ran as a serial in *Blackwood's* and was as eagerly looked for as a breath-taking novel. Next Noyes was asked by an editor, R. C. Lehman, to contribute to the *Speaker*, which was a leading liberal weekly. Noyes happened to be the first to mention the genius of G. K. Chesterton, whose work he reviewed. This made the two authors good friends.

Alfred Noyes was lucky in his literary life. He never knew the hardships, the continual disappointments and sometimes years of frustration from which most poets suffer. In 1907 he married an American girl, Garnett Daniels; and in 1913, six years later, he, with his wife, made his first visit to the United States. He had been asked to deliver the Lowell lectures at

Harvard and from 1914 to 1923 was professor of modern English literature at Princeton, excepting one year when he was working for the British Foreign Office.

Noyes tried to do his duty by his country when World War I came, but enlistment was impossible because of his poor eyesight. So he endeavored to use both his pen and his voice in his country's service. He was made a Companion of the British Empire in 1918—one of the highest of honors. So his efforts were crowned. But he lost his wife soon afterward. In 1927 he married again, a widow, Mary Weld-Blundell, and had three children, a son and two daughters. His later years were happy ones in spite of his almost total loss of sight. He had many gratifications and was honored in his work; he met all the great of his day. Having written lyrics and stirring ballads, he turned to other veins and wrote books on history, biography and controversial subjects. His play *Sherwood, or Robin Hood and the Three Kings* was produced in London in 1927 and his *Tales of Old Japan* was set to music as a cantata. Among his best-known books are: *Drake, Tales of the Mermaid Tavern, The Torch Bearers, The Watchers of the Sky, The Book of the Earth, The Last Voyage.*

Noyes was a tall, rather heavy-set man, clean shaven, with thin sandy hair, a brisk manner and a serious expression. On the whole he resembled a business man more than a poet. His homes alternated between Hanover Square, London, and St. Lawrence on the Isle of Wight, where he bought Lisle Combe, a house with an exquisite garden. Here he knew and cared for every tree, shrub and flower and, despite his blindness, could find his way among them on his various walks. It was on the Isle of Wight that he died in 1958 after a full life. Part One of "The Highwayman" is quoted here:

THE HIGHWAYMAN

The wind was a torrent of darkness among the gusty trees,
The moon was a ghostly galleon tossed upon cloudy seas,
The road was a ribbon of moonlight over the purple moor,
And the highwayman came riding—
      Riding—riding—
The highwayman came riding, up to the old inn-door.

He'd a French cocked-hat on his forehead, a bunch of lace at his
    chin,
A coat of the claret velvet and breeches of brown doe-skin;
They fitted with never a wrinkle: his boots were up to the thigh!
And he rode with a jeweled twinkle.
      His pistol butts a-twinkle,
His rapier hilt a-twinkle, under the jeweled sky.

Over the cobbles he clattered and clashed in the dark inn-yard,
And he tapped with his whip on the shutters, but all was locked
    and barred;
He whistled a tune to the window, and who should be waiting
    there
But the landlord's black-eyed daughter,
      Bess, the landlord's daughter,
Plaiting a dark-red love-knot into her long black hair.

And dark in the dark old inn-yard a stable-wicket creaked
Where Tim, the ostler listened; his face was white and peaked;
His eyes were hollows of madness, his hair like mouldy hay,
But he loved the landlord's daughter,
      The landlord's red-lipped daughter;
Dumb as a dog he listened, and he heard the robber say—

"One kiss, my bonny sweetheart, I'm after a prize tonight,
But I shall be back with the yellow gold before the morning light;

Yet, if they press me sharply and harry me through the day,
Then look for me by moonlight,
   Watch for me by moonlight,
I'll come to thee by moonlight, though hell should bar the way."

He rose upright in the stirrups; he scarce could reach her hand
But she loosened her hair i' the casement! His face burnt like
   a brand
As the black cascade of perfume came tumbling over his breast;
And he kissed its waves in the moonlight,
   (Oh, sweet black waves in the moonlight!)
Then he tugged at his reins in the moonlight and galloped away
   to the West.

ROBERT FROST

[1875–1963]

ROBERT FROST, for many years our loved poet laureate of the American scene, was born on March 26, 1875, in San Francisco, California, of New England and Scotch parentage. His father was William Prescott Frost; his mother, Margaret Moodie. His father edited a Democratic newspaper and, having taken the Southern side in the War between the States, named his son Robert Lee Frost for General Lee whom he greatly admired. The father died when the son was ten, and the mother with her children came East to live with her father in Lawrence, Massachusetts.

Homesick for California, young Robert began adjusting to a totally different life in a new land. His mother read aloud to him a great deal and his favorite book was *Tom Brown's Schooldays*. By the time he was fifteen he had gone on to Emerson, Bryant and Poe. One thing was absolutely clear in his mind. He would be a poet and had already begun to compose his own verses.

The first poem, which he sold at seventeen, was "My Butterfly." It was published in a magazine, the *Independent*, and he was paid fifteen dollars for it. William Hayes Ward, the editor, tried hard to induce the young poet to change his style—but this he would not do. Frost won high honors when he was graduated from the Lawrence, Massachusetts, high school and was asked to deliver the valedictory address. But there was a certain girl in his class, Elinor Miriam White, who was doing four years' work in two and a half years—and her marks were higher than his. The teachers decided to put Elinor White and Robert Frost down on the program as sharing the valedictory.

Robert went on to Dartmouth College but did not stay. Instead he offered himself as a bobbin boy in a mill. He then had time to read, to think and to talk with the farmers and village characters. In this way he caught the turn of their speech and absorbed their point of view. When he was twenty he married Elinor White, the girl with whom he had shared the valedictory at school. She was not only a help but an inspiration to him. He tried many trades. By turns he was a country schoolteacher, a cobbler, a small-town editor on the *St. Lawrence Sentinel* and at one time a farmer near Derry, New Hampshire, where his grandfather bought him a farm. But the soil was stony and the experiment a failure.

When the Frosts had acquired four children and Robert had difficulty in placing his poems, the family suddenly decided to go to England for a time. It was a shot in the dark but a wise move. As if by magic Frost's work was recognized and he made warm friends among the English poets, especially Rupert Brooke and Edward Thomas, both of whom died in World War I. After the Frosts returned to America there was recognition of his work in this country and Frost's books were published, although they made little money. At intervals life was still a struggle. But finally honors came his way.

Four times Robert Frost won the Pulitzer Prize for a book of poems. He won the Loines prize in 1931, the Mark Twain medal in 1937, the gold medal of the National Institute Academy of Arts and Letters in 1939, the gold medal of the Edward MacDowell Association and the Bollingen prize immediately before his death on January 29, 1963.

When young people read Frost's poems they get the smell of loam in a field, the feel of a snow-laden forest, the scent of apples in an apple picking. He is unquestionably the poet and philosopher of New England and has no rival in his own especial field. His principal books are: *A Boy's Will* (1913); *North of Boston* (1914); *Mountain Interval* (1916); *New Hampshire* (1923); *West-Running Brook* (1928); *Collected Poems* (1930); *A Further Range* (1936); *A Witness Tree* (1942); *Come in, and Other Poems* (1943); *Steeple Bush* (1947); *The Road Not Taken* (1951); *You Come Too,* (1959); *In the Clearing* (1962).

CARL SANDBURG

[1878–   ]

Carl sandburg was born in Galesburg, Illinois, the son of August Sandburg and Clara Matilda Anderson. His parents came from Swedish peasant stock. His father never learned to write his name but made a mark instead and read with much effort. He was a blacksmith in the shops of the Chicago, Burlington and Quincy Railroad, a sober, excellent mechanic who took care of a wife and seven children on fourteen cents an hour for a ten-hour day. He was swindled in the matter of the first house he bought with all his savings—eight hundred dollars—and Carl, a little boy of six, felt this deeply. In consequence all his life he championed the poor and helpless. When Carl beat up the Irish boys in some fracas, his father would rap "Sharley," as he was called at home, over the head with his tough knuckles and say he would come to no good end. Though his name was Carl August it was changed to Charles August and his friends and comrades called him Cully.

When he had finished eighth grade at thirteen, Carl had to go to work and his first job was driving a milk wagon. He used to recite his favorite verse and prose while he drove the wagon. He was especially fond of Gray's "Elegy" and the Bible, and he sang and recited poetry while he worked. In his teens he longed to be a potter, loving the feel of the clay between his fingers. But when he was porter and bootblack at Humphrey's barber shop, he was happy because he could listen to the customers' talk about local history and politics. Galesburg's real hero was always Lincoln, and the town, strongly Republican, had citizens who remembered shaking hands with him. Two bronze plaques placed beside the doors of Old Main Hall commemorated Lincoln and Douglas's fourth debate held there. No wonder Sandburg in his maturity was to honor Lincoln.

When Carl was seventeen, his brother and older sister lent him what money they could and he left town to be a writer and if not a writer, then a hobo. But of course he had to return. When the Spanish-American War broke out, he enlisted and did excellent service. His letters from the front to the home paper were his first published work. When he came back, he entered Lombard College in September 1898 and the college gave him free tuition for one year. He was offered an appointment to the U.S. Military Academy, but owing to his lack of schooling, he could not pass the examinations in arithmetic or grammar. So back to Lombard College he went and during his second year there rang the bell for classes to pay his expenses. Then during his junior and senior years he served as janitor for the Galesburg Fire Department and that paid all college fees. But though Carl Sandburg had four full years of college, this strange boy never took the diploma which awaited him. He wandered off by himself on the day of graduation.

But there was a professor of English at Lombard named Philip Green Wright who took an interest in this raw boy and was an influence in his life. Wright printed fifty copies of Sandburg's first little book on his own private printing press. The book was a collection of poetry and prose called

In Reckless Ecstasy and dedicated to Carl's mother. Wright knew that Carl was reading everything—Boccaccio, Walt Whitman, Emerson and Tolstoi—besides every book in the Lombard College Library that dealt with Lincoln and Lincoln's times. His college mates called Sandburg "that terrible Swede." Sometimes, like Vachel Lindsay, he walked over the prairie country, selling stereoscopic views and strumming on a guitar. He became aware of America in the songs of her farm hands, cowboys, rivermen, Negro stevedores as well as the workers in her stockyards. On leaving his native town in 1906 he never came back except as a visitor.

In the summer of 1907–8, while he was a paid party organizer of the Social-Democratic party in Milwaukee, Carl fell in love with Lillian Paula Steichen and they were married in 1908. Now the roving poet could no longer roam. He became a feature writer for many Milwaukee papers and shifted his job many times. Once when he lost work he had to address envelopes, as he now had a wife and baby to support. Only in odd moments could he write his poems. His second book was *Chicago Poems* (1916 and he soon had another one called *Cornhuskers* (1918). He had absorbed and become the literal voice of the prairie country and began contributing to Harriet Monroe's new magazine, *Poetry*. In 1914 he won its Levinson prize of two hundred dollars for a series of poems on the Chicago scene to be published in that magazine and to be called "Chicago." In 1920 he shared the same prize with Stephen Vincent Benét for his *Smoke and Steel. Slabs of the Sunburnt West* was published in 1922 and *Good Morning, America* in 1928. His *Rootabaga Stories* for children were modern fairy tales. Meanwhile in boxes and boxes he was gradually collecting his material on Lincoln and over sixteen years the many volumes made their appearance. In his garret workshop on the Michigan farm he got his material for *The War Years* slowly into shape. It was published in 1943 and won its author the Pulitzer Prize for history. His old college, Lombard, gave a degree in literature to the ex-student who went away without his diploma, and Harvard and Yale each gave him an honorary doctorate.

As the poet of the prairie, Sandburg is a hard-working, simple man who came up from humble beginnings. His poem called "Prairie" all children will love as it gives a tremendously real description of the land as he knew it in his youth. He has a happy home life with his wife and daughters and the house resounds to his laughter when he is there. He has one peculiarity—the penknife. Harry Golden says in his book, *Carl Sandburg*, "He has penknives all over the house and carries at least two of them wherever he goes. When he sets up in some home or in a hotel as an overnight guest, the penknife goes out on the night table beside him. Over the years he's developed a habit of gazing into the windows of pawnshops, always looking for interesting penknives."

Sandburg says of life: "It's going to come out all right, do you know?"

HENRY WADSWORTH LONGFELLOW

[1807–1882]

H ENRY WADSWORTH LONGFELLOW, the poet who wrote "The Children's Hour," was born on February 27, 1807, in Portland, Maine, the son of Stephen Longfellow and Zilpah Wadsworth. Portland was a seafaring town and the house in which he was born looked out on the ocean. His mother was fond of poetry and music and taught him to love them. There were eight children, a large and happy family, and Stephen, the brother, two years older, was Henry's companion. They flew kites, played ball and went swimming. The Maine winters were bitter cold and their rooms were icy, but they would plunge into good deep feather beds and soon be warm as toast and sound asleep. The children enjoyed the circus which came to town occasionally and they had plenty of books. Henry's favorite stories were the *Arabian Nights* and *Robinson Crusoe*, and he was fond of *Don Quixote* and Irving's *Sketch Book*. Their mother read the Bible to them. When Henry was three years old he was sent to Ma'am Fellows' dame school. She was a disciplinarian and the children dared not smile in her presence. But at another school to which he was sent at six and a half Henry got a splendid certificate of character. The teacher wrote: "Master Henry Longfellow is one of the best boys we have in the school. He spells and reads very well. He also can add and multiply numbers. His conduct last quarter was very correct and amiable."

He was only fifteen when he entered Bowdoin College in Portland. He made the sophomore class and there he met Nathaniel Hawthorne, who became his close friend. While in college Henry Longfellow did a good deal of writing. Seventeen poems were finished and later on five of these were included in his books. When he graduated, at barely nineteen, he was awarded the honor of delivering one of the English orations. Next he was elected to the chair of modern languages. But the faculty required that he travel in Europe for three years to learn the languages he was to teach. When he returned for a short time in 1831 he married and went with his wife to Europe to continue the tour. Four years later she was suddenly taken ill and died abroad. This was a terrible blow, but he had to go on to fit himself for his new position. When he came back and was established at the college, he married again and very happily. He bought the old Craigie house and there were born his six children, three of whom are mentioned in "The Children's Hour," "grave Alice and laughing Allegra and Edith with golden hair." The poet's home life was ideal and did much for his writing. He was known as the Children's Poet. Hawthorne suggested to him that he should write the romantic story of "Evangeline" and that was followed by "Hiawatha," the poem that all school children know and love.

Longfellow lost his second wife tragically, but he persevered in the work that had become a joy to him. His books sold well and he could live on the income from them. On his last trip to Europe, when he was sixty, Longfellow, now the outstanding American poet, was heaped with honors. One day in London a laborer stood by his carriage, saying, "I wish to shake hands with the author of the "Psalm of Life."

His old age was a very happy one. On his seventy-second birthday the children of Cambridge gave him an armchair made out of the wood of the spreading chestnut tree in his poem on the "Village Blacksmith." It was black and carved with the fruit and leaves of the horse chestnut and upholstered in green leather. It had a brass plate beneath the cushion with the inscription, "To the Author of the *Village Blacksmith*, this chair made from the wood of the spreading chestnut tree is presented as an expression of grateful regard by the children of Cambridge. February 27th, 1879." A reply was sent to the children in the shape of a poem, "From My Armchair."

When Longfellow died at seventy-five he was greatly mourned by the whole land. He wrote in beautiful and musical English and there was an artistic quality to all his verse. He loved children and was loved by them.

INDEX

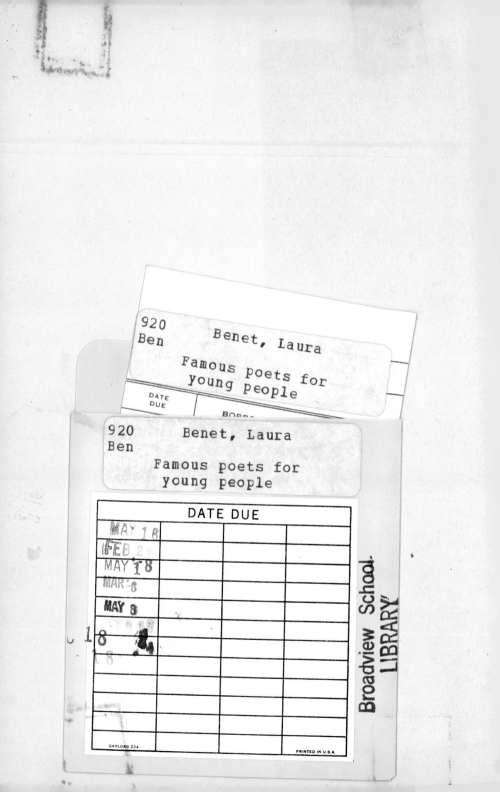